My Life for Yours

Look for more books in the Wilson Family Series:

by Douglas Wilson:

Reforming Marriage

Her Hand in Marriage

Standing on the Promises:
A Handbook on Biblical Childrearing

Fidelity:
What it Means to be a One-Woman Man

Federal Husband

Future Men

by Nancy Wilson:

The Fruit of Her Hands:
Respect and the Christian Woman

Praise Her in the Gates:
The Calling of Christian Motherhood

www.canonpress.org

My Life for Yours

A Walk though the Christian Home

DOUGLAS WILSON

CANON PRESS
MOSCOW, IDAHO

Douglas J. Wilson, *My Life for Yours: A Walk through the Christian Home*
© 2004 by Douglas J. Wilson.

Published by Canon Press, P.O. Box 8741, Moscow, ID 83843
800–488–2034 / www.canonpress.org

05 06 07 08 09 10 / 10 9 8 7 6 5 4 3 2 1

Cover design by Paige Atwood

Cover painting: Yuon, Konstantin (1875-1958); Evening in August.
Location: Tretyakov Gallery, Moscow, Russia
Photo Credit: Scala/Art Resource, NY

Printed in the United States of America.

Unless otherwise noted, Scripture quotations are taken from the Autho-
rized Version.

Library of Congress Cataloging-in-Publication Data

Wilson, Douglas
  My life for yours : a walk through the Christian home / Douglas J.
Wilson.
     p. cm.
  Includes index.
  ISBN 1-885767-90-0 (pbk.)
  1. Family—Religious life. 2. Family—Religious aspects—Christianity.
I. Title.

BV4526.3.W55 2004
248.4—dc22   2004000915

Table of Contents

Introduction

Welcome to another book on the family, one that covers the perennial issues of the home from another vantage point.

The origins of this book are somewhat eclectic. I preached a series of sermons on this theme and wrote most of the chapters around the sermon outlines. The sermonic and pointed nature of the second-person plural address is still visible (I hope), while at the same time becoming formal enough to warrant having a justified margin. "The Junk Drawer" chapter is taken from a series of email meditations, entitled *Grace and Peace*, sent out to our church on a weekly basis.

I am particularly grateful to Thomas Howard, who wrote a fine book a number of years ago following the same poetic conceit—that of working through all the rooms of the house. His book was entitled *Splendor in the Ordinary* and was a very helpful and edifying work. Those who haunt used book stores would do well to keep an eye out for it. Though we follow the same conceit, and his house apparently had a lot of the same rooms that mine does, the differences still are worth noting. His Roman Catholic trajectory was evident even at that time, just as I trust that my Puritan trajectory is in evidence here. At the same time, as one mere Christian to another, I owe him for the wonderful phrase, *my life for yours*.

CHAPTER ONE

The Front Porch and Door

*And thou shalt write them upon the door posts of thine
house, and upon thy gates: That your days may be
multiplied, and the days of your children, in the land
which the* LORD *sware unto your fathers to give them,
as the days of heaven upon the earth.* (Deut. 11:20–21)

As Christians, our central concern should be to have our
worship of God pervade everything we do. But if worship
applied relates to how we live, then it must also relate to
where we live. The goal of this book, therefore, is to work
through every room of the house, seeing what we discover
there in the light of the Scriptures. And we will start on the
front porch, just outside the door.

We see in the text above the importance of an overt and
visible dedication of the home to God and His Word. This
dedication to God is not to be a compartmentalized affair—
that is, it's not limited to one room in the house or to one
day of the week. The claims of God are always *total*, which
can be seen on the doorposts.

The dedication and design of the Temple (1 Kgs. 6:3;
1 Chr. 28:11) extended from the porch to the altar
(Joel 2:17). In the same way, the dedication of our homes
to Christ includes the porch and the front door as an important symbol. Slaves were dedicated permanently at the
door (Exod. 21:6). Aaron and his sons were consecrated at
the door of the tabernacle (Exod. 29:4). The ascension
(consecration) offerings were closely associated with the

door of the tabernacle (Exod. 29:42). The tithes were col-
lected at the door (2 Kgs. 12:9). A wonderful conjunction
of this symbolism is found when God was worshipped at
the door of the tabernacle by every man in the door of his
tent.

> And it came to pass, when Moses went out unto
> the tabernacle, that all the people rose up, and stood
> every man at his tent door, and looked after Moses,
> until he was gone into the tabernacle. And it came
> to pass, as Moses entered into the tabernacle, the
> cloudy pillar descended, and stood at the door of
> the tabernacle, and the LORD talked with Moses. And
> all the people saw the cloudy pillar stand at the
> tabernacle door: and all the people rose up and wor-
> shipped, every man in his tent door. (Exod. 33:8–10)

As Christians, we ascend to the gates of heaven in our
worship on the Lord's Day. As we do, one greater than
Moses goes before us. As we consider this, an important
question for us to keep in mind is this: are we worshipping
rightly *from the doors of our homes?* Doors are a place of
dedication, and so it's fitting for us to begin our consideration of how we are to live together as Christians at the
front door.

GRACE AND LAW
Christians are often unnecessarily bothered by the relationship of grace and law. But the preface to the Ten Commandments is actually a wonderful statement of *grace*. God
had brought them up out of the house of bondage, and then
afterwards He graciously gave them His law. It's the same
kind of thing here. We show our allegiance to God and His
word by displaying His law on the doorposts of the house.
But in the households of Israel, these were the same doorposts where the blood of the Passover lamb had been placed.

And they shall take of the blood, and strike it on the two side posts and on the upper door post of the houses, wherein they shall eat it. (Exod. 12:7; cf., 22–23)

First the blood, then the law. It's the same in the New Covenant—first the blood of Christ, and then the word of that same Christ. The one who gave Himself for us as a sacrifice is the same one who speaks to us as our Lord. So, while the law on the doorposts shows we are dedicated to God, the blood (that was there first) shows we are a house of *forgiven sinners* dedicated to God. Because Christ is our Paschal sacrifice and our high priest, it follows that He is also our prophet and our king. And all these realities are seen, though in a figure, at our front door.

A FALLEN WORLD

In this world, corrupted as it is by sin, and threatened by sin, doors and gates are a necessary protection. In the heavenly Jerusalem, the Church, such protections are not necessary (Rev. 21:25; Is. 60:11), but short of that glory they always are (Ezek. 38:11; Jer. 49:31). When the residents of Sodom threatened his guests, Lot guarded them at the door, and he guarded them with the door (Gen. 19:6). When God destroyed the antediluvian world with the Flood, the distinction between the inside of the ark and the outside of it was the most important distinction on earth, and that distinction was sealed and marked with the door (Gen. 6:16). A door protects us against the weather and against intruders.

A door therefore speaks of protection. In this respect, it is a symbol of the husband and father. Just as God placed Adam in the garden to tend and keep it, assigning him the priestly task of protection, in the same way husbands should exercise their responsibility to be a door of protection for their families. Adam failed in his duty, and we see the tragic consequences of a husband who is a broken door, hanging from one hinge.

Wives need to know that their husbands are a door of protection for them. Children need to grow up in the kind of security that only a stout door can provide. Because it's a fallen world, because Adam was not the door he ought to have been, fathers today need to give this gift to their children.

WHO BELONGS?

A door marks the place where those who *belong* are free to enter. Jesus taught that thieves and robbers seek other means of entry than a door. In that context, He was speaking of salvation, but the principle remains an important one. Those whose presence is life-giving come through the door. Those who intend harm avoid the door (Jn. 10:1–2,7–10). We see this principle also in the parable of the foolish virgins (Mt. 25:10). A shut door excludes those who don't belong.

Those who come through the door are therefore *family* in some sense. They may be family by blood because they came through the organic door of birth. They may be family as extended guests (boarders), or they may simply be family for an evening (dinner guests). But if they came through the door, biblical hospitality means that all are gathered in some kind of family. Hosts and guests together *belong*. Because this is so, we are therefore to keep our own doors and respect the doors of others. Job says that if he violated the doorway of a neighbor then his house in turn should be violated.

> If mine heart have been deceived by a woman, or if I have laid wait at my neighbor's door; Then let my wife grind unto another, and let others bow down upon her. For this is an heinous crime; yea, it is an iniquity to be punished by the judges. For it is a fire that consumeth to destruction, and would root out all mine increase. (Job 31:9–12)

WIPE YOUR FEET

But family does not mean pandemonium. Doors are guarded against intruders, as we saw earlier. But doors are also guarded against the wear and tear brought by family—by people who belong. We need order and hierarchy in order to be able to live together, and it's important to note that while the Bible teaches the husband is the head of the wife, and the head of the house*hold*, in a very real sense the wife is the head of the *house*. This is something which should be very clear to everyone in the home, and it should be clear at the *door*.

The apostle Paul says this: "I will therefore that the younger women marry, bear children, guide the house, give none occasion to the adversary to speak reproachfully" (1 Tim. 5:14). The phrase "guide the house" is a translation of one Greek word which literally rendered (in its form as a noun) would be *house-despot*. The apostle says something similar elsewhere. "That they may teach the young women to be sober, to love their husbands, to love their children, to be discreet, chaste, keepers at home, good, obedient to their own husbands, that the word of God be not blasphemed (Tit. 2:4–5). "Keepers at home" renders one word which would literally be *home-guard*.

How is this first word (*oikodespotes*) used elsewhere in Scripture? Some of the other uses show clearly the idea of a true and functioning *authority* (Mt. 10:25; 13:27, 52; 20:1, 11; 21:33; 24:43). The idea of a wife as live-in maid or all-purpose drudge is antithetical to the scriptural pattern. The woman of the house is the mistress of her domain (and it is *her* domain); she has authority that can and should be exercised over the members of that household. This extends to issues great and small: The laundry goes here, shoes come off at the door, rinse the dishes before they go in the dishwasher.

And so I want to say something here which could easily be misunderstood or misrepresented, but it's still necessary. A husband as the head of his wife is an honored and permanent guest, but he should learn to see himself *as a guest.* Another way of saying this is that one of a husband's central duties is that of providing his wife with a domain where she exercises the kind of authority you see throughout that famous Proverbs 31 passage. One of the striking things about conservative Christians is how often they can cite that passage without paying attention to just exactly what is going on in it. That woman, whose price is above rubies, works in real estate, manages a vineyard, manufactures textiles, labors as a seamstress, works as a philanthropist, and directs all the servant girls. In short, she is the very model of an *oikodespotes.*

Just as God gave Adam a garden to tend and keep, so a husband is to provide his wife with a garden to tend and keep. This is no pretence; there is genuine delegation and genuine responsibility involved in this. And the authority of the woman over the house should be apparent at the front gate of the yard and the front door of the house.

WISDOM AND FOLLY

The way we are with God at the center will be evident in the *precincts* of our lives. This is certainly the case with the foolish woman of Proverbs. "A foolish woman is clamorous: she is simple, and knoweth nothing. For *she sitteth at the door of her house*, on a seat in the high places of the city" (Prov. 9:13–14). Because this is the case, we are to recognize from a distance how things are and stay away. "Remove thy way far from her, and come not nigh the door of her house" (Prov. 5:8). We are not to seek to go through the doors of folly; we should not desire to be guests in any kind of house when sin and folly are emblazoned at the door.

In a similar way, we guard our own doors with all wisdom, seeking to prevent sin from encroaching. We should keep the warning to Cain in mind: "If thou doest well, shalt thou not be accepted? and if thou doest not well, sin lieth at the door. And unto thee shall be his desire, and thou shalt rule over him" (Gen. 4:7).

Everyone here should want to say with Joshua, "as for me and my house, we will serve the LORD" (Josh. 24:15). And this service begins at the door.

CHAPTER TWO

The Living Room

If there be therefore any consolation in Christ, if any comfort of love, if any fellowship of the Spirit, if any bowels and mercies, Fulfil ye my joy, that ye be likeminded, having the same love, being of one accord, of one mind. Let nothing be done through strife or vainglory; but in lowliness of mind let each esteem other better than themselves. Look not every man on his own things, but every man also on the things of others. (Phil. 2:1–4)

In addressing our subject of the biblical home in this way, we are not making the assumption that the layout of modern homes is identical to the homes of biblical times or even that modern homes are identical to one another. At the same time, we *are* assuming a large degree of human commonality—such that applications can readily be made despite the various differences we all recognize. When Christ told the story about the sower who broadcast his seed by hand, He was not assuming His story would become irrelevant when someone invented some other way of sowing seed. That said, we come to the living room.

In this passage, Paul calls upon the Philippians to take what they have been given—their consolation in Christ, their comfort of love, their fellowship of the Spirit, their tendermercies—and to do something with it (2:1). What they are to do is fulfill the apostle's joy, cultivate likemindedness, share their love, and be of one accord and one mind

(Phil. 2:2). Negatively, they are to repudiate entirely the attitude which is antithetical to this, an attitude given to strife and vainglory. Rather, in lowliness of mind, which is humility, they are to esteem others more important than themselves (2:3). Each person is to look out for the others first (2:4). Paul goes on in this glorious passage to show how Jesus Christ Himself was the archetypical pattern for this.

WHAT YOU ARE AT HOME

What a man is at home is what that same man is at church. Who a woman is at home is who she is at church. Character doesn't change with an alteration in the longitude and latitude. But this is not the same thing as what *others* may think you are at church. Weekly hypocrisy puts a strain on a carnal man, but the thing can still be done. A praise-the-Lord smile can always be ginned up by the time you get to church, leaving the thunderstruck kids wondering why non-family members get the gracious treatment, and they get snarled at in the car on the way. Paul's injunction can only be obeyed in the family of the saints, in the household of faith, if it's already being obeyed at home in the various families of that congregation.

The living room, unlike most other rooms in the house, does not have an obvious *physical* function. A kitchen is where food is prepared, a dining room is where it's eaten, and bedrooms are for sleeping. But what is a living room *for*? The name indicates the answer—it is for *living*. This means conversation, reading, resting, napping, and other assorted activities. And all such activities are to be built on the bedrock of humble sacrifice. As mentioned earlier, the central principle of godly living in a Christian home is the principle of "my life for yours." This means love and humility and is what makes a living room a *living* room. In what room of the house should you give your *life* away? Well, of course, in all of them, but what room is particularly suited for this? A life should be offered in the living room.

But because we are not gnostics, we need to recognize that there is more to this than simply trying to accomplish an "attitude adjustment." Paul tells us to present our bodies as a living sacrifice (Rom. 12:1–2), and there are practical ways to do this that relate to the architecture of the living room.

The wife is responsible for the home, as we noted in the previous chapter. Among other duties, this includes the responsibility for decorating and arranging the home, including the living room. Some basic thoughts are important.

First is the question of *tone*. The central attitude, again, is "my life for yours." Just as the husband is to serve others, so the wife is to serve others. There is a vast difference between a woman's touch, which is most necessary, and what might be called "foofiness" on steroids. There are times when frilly surroundings make the males of the house feel like strangers in a strange land.

There is also the practical question of *layout*. If there is a desire for something to be central, then it's necessary to *arrange for it*. Conversely, if the desire is keep something away from the spiritual center, then it would be wise to not put it at the physical center. There is a vast difference, for example, between a living room arranged for conversation and a living room arranged for television watching. Promote what you want to promote.

Then there is the necessity of *trade-offs*. Someone has to maintain the living room—tidying, vacuuming, and so forth. And the mistress of the domain has the authority to establish certain house rules which are simply wise preventative measures. But the goal—*living* together—should not be forgotten by anyone. Wiping your feet or taking off your shoes is one thing, but sometimes people have to take their shoes off at the end of the driveway, the furniture is covered with those attractive plastic sheets with little bumps on them, and the room itself is cordoned off with velvet ropes that make you think Thomas Jefferson might have been born in there. "Where no oxen are, the crib is clean: but much increase is by the strength of the ox" (Prov. 14:4). What is the *point*? A living room should be lived in.

LIFE AND DEATH

When Scripture calls for discussion of the things of God when we lie down, when we rise up, when we walk along the road, and so on, it does so presupposing a life *together* (Deut. 6:4–9). In our homes, the center of this life together is the living room. What are some of the temptations that lead us away from this?

One of them is the pressure for *abandonment*. After a quick dinner, if there is a dinner at all, the family scatters to the four winds. Back to their bedrooms, off to some activity, the family scatters like the lost tribes of Israel. If this is the case, father and mother should *not* rush to fix this by decree or fiat. Why does the family not *want* to be together? It might be bad attitudes, it might be simple laziness and drift that have led to a bad habit, or it might be that the living room simply doesn't have room for everyone to sit down. If it's the former kind of thing, then restoration should begin with confession of responsibility and sin. If the latter, then it should be addressed with a simple rearrangement of furniture and schedules.

The family might not scatter, but rather they might be all together facing in an odd direction. In this case, the family does do things together, but too much of it is shoulder to shoulder, watching something unrelated to them all. There is too little face-to-face time, too little visiting or conversation. Obviously, this doesn't mean a family cannot watch a movie together which can be wonderful fodder of great conversation afterwards. But a problem does exist if the family watches something together and *then* everyone immediately scatters. This means they were watching the movie "together" simply because the family is not well off enough to have a DVD player in every bedroom. Here, as with so many other issues, it's important to remember the principle. Wooden applications of any of these principles, made in a panic, won't fix anything. The point is to structure the living room so that it's *conducive* to genuine relationship.

Unfortunately, there is also the problem that could be called a *hellish perversion*. If parents browbeat their children, they cannot be surprised if resentments set in. Mandatory "family times"—togetherness by dictatorial decree—do nothing but chain the kids to the problem. But the right sense of *mandatory* can be seen when the kids don't let the parents skip the time, stop the reading, or whatever. I can recall evenings when my family would not permit me to stop the after-dinner reading (*The Lord of the Rings*, as I remember), and I had to go for two or three hours. It was mandatory family time, all right. It was mandatory for *me*.

That which is intended for life must never be made the instrument of death. We are never to boil a kid in its mother's milk (Deut. 14:21).

THE CROWN OF HUMILITY

We are all sinners, and this sin will be manifested from time to time in the living room. The point is not that the presence of any sin means the family cause is hopeless. God knew we were sinners when He put us together in the first place. This is a *design* feature, and it means life together in such a way that recognizes how God deals with sin—that is, with the blood of Christ appropriated by the gift of repentance and faith.

And this brings us back to the beginning. In the living room, because we are living together, learning how to live in one accord, let nothing be done in strife or vainglory. Sinners who live together cannot afford to be proud.

CHAPTER THREE

Unwanted Guests: Pride

Love not the world, neither the things that are in the world. If any man love the world, the love of the Father is not in him. For all this is in the world, the lust of the flesh, and the lust of the eyes, and the pride of life, is not of the Father, but is of the world. And the world passeth away, and the lust thereof: but he that doeth the will of God abideth for ever. (1 Jn. 2:15–17)

In the garden, giving way to "all that is in the world," the woman saw that the tree was good for food, pleasant to the eyes, and able to make one wise (Gen. 3:6). Every sin that can be committed is traceable back to pride. Boil all the sinful meat off, and what you have left are the bones of pride. This is how we may summarize worldliness: belly, eyes, and fevered brains. But why do people persist in sin? Why do they persist in sin in a Christian home? The answer is found in the last culprit named by John—the pride of life.

We all understand the temptations that overthrow us when we were not premeditating any disobedience. We did not *plan* to lose our tempers, feel that envious pang, or give way to lust. It just happened, as we tell ourselves later. But why do we refuse to apologize? Or confess? Or make restitution? And why does that refusal extend over hours, days, weeks, and years? The answer here is *pride*, and this ongoing sin *is* premeditated.

A husband and father who loses his temper with his family has committed the sin of anger. But if he refuses to seek explicit forgiveness from everyone he has wronged, in a manner just as public as the sin was, he is no longer guilty of just the sin of anger. He is now living in unconfessed sin—the sin of stubborn pride. He may think the storm is passed, but the rest of the family is not so foolish. They see the standing pride, and the attitude of pride, the unwillingness to humble himself.

This is a sin that God hates above all others. Six things God hates, seven are loathsome to Him. What is first on the list?

> These six things doth the LORD hate: yea, seven are an abomination unto him: a proud look, a lying tongue, and hands that shed innocent blood" (Prov. 6:16–17)

Murder of innocents is *third* on the list, and a nose in the air is number *one*. The Lord condemns it as proceeding, with other sins, from a filthy heart (Mk. 7:22–23). God insults the very appearance of the proud (Ps. 73:6–7). He really does hate it.

And yet many Christian parents have somehow come to believe that this sin is acceptable within their homes.

How does God describe the prideful?

> Behold, this was the iniquity of thy sister Sodom, pride, fulness of bread, and abundance of idleness was in her and in her daughters, neither did she strengthen the hand of the poor and needy. (Ezek. 16:49)

When we think of the sin of Sodom, we often forget the central sin, the cause of all the other problems. The great problem with Sodom was not sodomy but pride. The sexual perversion was a later development; the pride was first. And yet, there are many staunch Christian parents who are outraged at sins like sodomy, but they nurture the mother of this perversion around their own dining room tables. They defend it; they cherish it. It is their *precious*. Prideful people do not consider the poor and needy, and in a family, the children are the poor and needy. But pride does not care.

And consider the same thing from another angle:

> The wicked in his pride doth persecute the poor: let them be taken in the devices that they have imagined. For the wicked boasteth of his heart's desire, and blesseth the covetous, whom the LORD abhorreth. The wicked, through the pride of his countenance, will not seek after God: God is not in all his thoughts." (Ps. 10:2–4)

According to the Bible, the proud have contempt for the lowly, and so God has contempt for them in *their* lowliness. Children are lowly, and children of prideful parents are particularly vulnerable, but proud parents don't care that they are destroying their children.

God hates pride and so should we. What wisdom hates we should hate: "The fear of the LORD is to hate evil: pride, and arrogancy, and the evil way, and the froward mouth, do I hate" (Prov. 8:13). We sometimes think that we should not hate, but this is to reject the words of God. We must hate sins, and, if this is true, we must hate the mother of sins—pride, arrogance, insolence. And, of course, it should go without saying that we should hate it the most when it appears in our own hearts.

Not surprisingly, God does not leave pride alone. "And I will break the pride of your power; and I will make your heaven as iron, and your earth as brass" (Lev. 26:19). Pride is followed by shame because God sees to it. "When pride cometh, then cometh shame: but with the lowly is wisdom" (Prov. 11:2). Shame follows pride, and God wants it this way. Pride is the way to destruction. A proud man in his family will be brought low. A proud woman will be humbled. The Bible is plain here as well. "A man's pride shall bring him low: but honour shall uphold the humble in spirit" (Prov. 29:23). Of course, we also remember the famous passage—"Pride goeth before destruction, and an haughty spirit before a fall" (Prov. 16:18).

Speaking of church office, Paul mentions this in his discussions of elder qualifications. He says, "not a novice, lest being lifted up with pride he fall into the condemnation of the devil" (1 Tim. 3:6). Husbands and wives should consider that these are also offices, and as parents they hold an additional office. Pride is unbecoming and grotesque in any official, particularly when that office is an office in the home.

Many who read these words hold to the doctrines of the Reformed faith, as do I, but we must prayerfully consider the issue of doctrinal pride. "*We* have the truth!" When it comes to the doctrines of grace, this is particularly insane. What do we have that we did not receive as a gift? (1 Cor. 4:7). Moreover, it was a gift we emphatically did not want. This must be stated with great emphasis before the next point can be made.

The pride of man must always bow before the Godness of God. What happened when Nebuchanezzar's understanding returned to him? What did he say? Understanding who God is and gladly submitting to Him should be our very definition of what it means to be sane (Dan. 4:34–37). A sane father, a sane husband, a sane wife, a sane mother—these are all people who treasure in their hearts a remembrance of *who God is*.

What is the antidote to pride? The Bible teaches that the answer is *boasting*. "My soul shall make her boast in the LORD: the humble shall hear thereof, and be glad" (Ps. 34:2; cf., 2 Cor. 10:17). We are prideful because we do not boast enough—in the Lord, that is.

In our homes, as we learn to boast in the Lord, we will be learning simultaneously to humble ourselves. There will be no incongruity in a father seeking forgiveness from his children or in a wife seeking forgiveness from her husband publicly at the dinner table because that's where she made her disrespectful comment. Children who are taught to confess their sins—to God, to parents, to siblings—will not resent this because their parents are teaching them to do something that they have also lived out by example. If this is not happening, then the foundation of the household is pride, and God will bring it down.

WHEN PRIDE RULES

One of the great sorrows that comes upon many wives and children is the sorrow of *needing* protection from the one that should be *doing* the protecting. When this is a settled state of affairs, the problem is always one of stubbornness and pride.

When pride rules, authority is wielded poorly. But in talking about authorities in the home doing poorly, we are not talking about parents or husbands who simply sin. Sin is present in every home; the question concerns what we are to do about it. God's covenant with man takes sin into account, and faithfulness includes availing oneself of the means He has supplied. The same thing is true in the covenant of the home. Parents living poorly places them under a disobedient authority. Wives with disobedient husbands are in the same position.

What should be done when the parents (or just one parent) or a husband will not deal with flagrant sin appropriately? As a child or a wife in such a home, it's necessary to trust God, acknowledging, first of all, you are not "stuck." It is a wise providence that has placed you where you are. In such a bad situation, your first task is to ensure that you are not an active part of the complex web of sinning yourself—by means of resentment, bitterness, provocations, and so on.

That done, if you are not a player, then you need to guard your heart against resentment, being prepared at all times to forgive if given the least opportunity. And last, you need to learn the enormous power of example that Peter urges for those in such situations (1 Pet. 3:1–6).

CHAPTER FOUR

Holidays in the Living Room

Wherefore they called these days Purim after the name of Pur. Therefore for all the words of this letter, and of that which they had seen concerning this matter, and which had come unto them, The Jews ordained, and took upon them, and upon their seed, and upon all such as joined themselves unto them, so as it should not fail, that they would keep these two days according to their writing, and according to their appointed time every year. (Est. 9:26–27)

And it was at Jerusalem the feast of the dedication, and it was winter. And Jesus walked in the temple in Solomon's porch. (Jn. 10:22)

For various reasons, difficult to explain, some Christians have a difficult time celebrating Christmas, Easter, and other holidays. Sometimes the reasons are theological, or perhaps it would be better to say *ideological* (strict regulativism run amok). Sometimes they are practical (anti-consumerism run amok). They have seen too many merchants treating the birth of Christ as the year's biggest cash cow, and they don't like it. So they bow out. And other times the reasons are historical or ethical (anti-Romanism run amok). And it has to be said at the outset (when such folks are not objecting to the essential *lawfulness* of such observance), they almost always have a point.

There are times when that point is driven too far and taken to extremes, causing those who differ with them to reject what they actually ought to listen to.

The lawfulness of celebrating holidays apart from an express commandment to do so can be seen in our two texts. Unlike Pentecost and Passover and the other festivals required by the law of the Old Testament, Purim was established to celebrate God's deliverance of the Jews in Persia. The book of Esther tells the story of how this festival came to be, but there is no command from God in the book anywhere that would require the observance of the festival. The festival of Hanukkah was established after the Maccabean revolt in the intertestamental period when the Temple was cleansed of the defilements it had suffered under Antiochus Epiphanes. This was called the feast of dedication or lights, which Jesus observed. So, with regard to the lawfulness of God's people marking such days of deliverance in a godly way, we should consider the thing settled. As the Second Helvetic Confession from the Reformation era put it, "Moreover, if in Christian liberty the churches religiously celebrate the memory of the Lord's nativity, circumcision, passion, resurrection, and of his ascension into heaven, and the sending of the Holy Spirit upon his disciples, *we approve of it highly.*"

But the fact that something is lawful does not mean that those who handle it are doing so lawfully. Marriage is lawful. Can it not be abused? Beer is lawful. Is there no such thing as drunkenness? Guns are lawful. Is there no such thing as being a bad shot? The mere fact that God-honoring practices like Christmas observances in the home are *lawful* doesn't mean that the thing is being celebrated rightly.

THE LORD'S DAY

As we consider what we should be doing with annual celebrations, we need to begin by emphasizing our *weekly* celebration of the Lord's Day. This is for two reasons. The first is doctrinal. If someone disparages a holy-day that God gave to us *directly*, but then permits himself to become a Christmas freak, then he really is guilty of substituting man's traditions for God's (Mk. 7:7–8). The highest priority should always go to what God has required first. No enemy of the sabbath can be a true friend of a true Christmas. No one who neglects the Lord's Day (a weekly Easter) can have a healthy interest in the annual Easter.

The second reason is more practical. We have a hard time resisting the influence of unbelievers on our celebrations like Christmas primarily because *we are out of shape*. We open our presents (just like the nonbelievers) and then we are at a loss about what to do next. But there is nothing like weekly celebration to prepare believers for celebratory joy in an annual event.

THE DAY HAS NO POWER

One of the great idols of our age is sentimentalism, and one of the times of year when the power of this idol is most evident is at times like Christmas. Note that the problem is not the existence of affections, or sentiment, but rather whether they speak with a voice of authority. When we make idols out of wood and stone, the problem is not the wood or stone. The problem is what we are doing with them.

But we are Christians, and we are *not* to have the "spirit of Christmas." Rather, we have the Spirit of *God*. When we assume that the spirit of Christmas has a power it in fact does not have, we are setting ourselves up for various holiday familial disasters. The sentimentalism of Dickens is part of the reason so many families have collisions and quarrels during the holidays, because it's assumed the time of year, the snowfall, or the decorations have the power to make your brother less selfish and your uncle less boorish. But Christmas in itself is not a means of grace. It's a holiday to be celebrated *in* the Spirit but is not a substitute *for* the Spirit.

This is why Christmas, by itself, will not keep one's grandfather from losing his temper, one's mother from being manipulative, or the children from being selfish and greedy, but for the person *who expected it to*, the whole thing is a great letdown. To anticipate that the spirit of the season, the Christmas tree in the living room, and the decorations at the mall might make everyone righteous is to ask from an earthly thing what only the Holy Spirit can do. For the one who sets up false expectations like this, the necessary result is real disappointment, and all the subsequent resentments that flow from it. The spirit of the holidays, whatever the holiday, is not the Spirit of God. Full understanding of this is necessary if Christian families are to avoid the perennial problem of holiday "scenes" or "showdowns."

GNOSTICISM AND PRESENTS

Another problem we face, particularly with Christmas, concerns the matter of gifts. Under the influence of gnosticism, we want to teach our children that it's not the gift that counts but rather the thought behind it. In doing this, we are teaching them to be gnostic ingrates (as distinguished from *materialist* ingrates). Rather, we should think incarnationally about the gifts we give and receive, and we should not try to make a separation between the giver and gift. We have been doing this for so long that we now have to try to not make a separation. Biblically understood, gifts are a way of extending *ourselves*. We do this in imitation of what God was doing for us in the Incarnation. God so loved, and so God gave. What would we make of a theologian who said the gift of Christ did not really matter, what mattered was the thought behind it? We would call it liberal tomfoolery and be done with it. So why do we imitate *that* theology?

Of course, God extends Himself in His gifts perfectly,

and we do not. This is an area where we need to grow in our sanctification, but we should have a clear idea of what direction we are going. When we give a gift rightly, we put a good deal of thought into the process precisely because we want the recipient to be excited about the *gift*. When someone we love is thrilled with what we got for them, that is in its turn a gift to the giver. This means that if we want to give back to the one who gives to us, one of the best ways to do this is through loving what they gave.

Few prospects are more dismal than a Christmas morning where everyone is trying to be what they think is spiritual. "Thank you for the tie, which I don't care for really at all, but which represents for me your constant love and affection." *God did not make the world this way.* Gifts are extensions of our personalities, and this is why we need to teach our children to give and receive, with gladness, wisdom, and excitement.

FOOD

We will of course address this in more detail when we come to the dining room, but holidays are one time of year when more food than usual makes its way out to the living room. Celebrations must have their special foods, drinks, desserts, and more. But there are pitfalls, particularly with fudge.

Actually, that was a joke, but there is an important principle to remember with food and that is *proportionality*. A wise family should not want any wild discrepancies in the celebration. For example, if by the time the ham gets to the table all the kitchen help are snarling at one another, then a central integrative point has been lost. You don't want the family to associate the best china with bitter family quarrels. If a family cannot celebrate with joy and gladness across the board, then somebody should order a pizza. It is better to have a dry morsel and quietness than feasting with strife (Prov. 17:1).

In addition to proportionality, there is also the

question of *propriety*. Holidays should be treated as festivals and not as fasts. The theme should be richness, and that means the aforementioned fudge. I *will* say (just once) that eating and drinking can be abused in the exuberant direction and that gluttony is a bad business. But that's not our temptation. The fat is the Lord's (Neh. 9:25). Especially at the holidays, a Christian family should let the table reflect a true theology of grace.

MUSIC AND THE WORD

As Christians celebrating in Christian homes, we should not expect the meaning of the symbols to communicate on their own. This means we should *talk* about them and *sing* about them. What does the laden table mean? The Christmas carols can tell us that. One of the most striking things about Christmas carols is how much truth they contain that most evangelical Christians don't believe, but we all sing annually anyway. He came to make His blessings flow far as the curse is found. *Really?* And what does the star on the top of the tree mean? Let Luke teach the family when you read the account aloud. What do the presents mean? Jesus was born to die in order that He might be born again from the dead—and us with Him.

CHAPTER FIVE

The Kitchen

For in Jesus Christ neither circumcision availeth any thing, nor uncircumcision; but faith which worketh by love. . . . For, brethren, ye have been called unto liberty; only use not liberty for an occasion to the flesh, but by love serve one another. (Gal. 5:6,13)

The constitution of a biblical home consists of faith, hope, and love, but the greatest of these is love. Love is not to be understood as mere sentiment, but rather self-sacrificing obedience to the Word of God—with a whole heart. This can be quite an elevating and inspiring concept until there are dishes to be done.

In a real sense, the kitchen is near the center of the home, and it's there as a place of *preparation*. It's not a room that exists for itself. In just the same way that clothes were not created for the washing machine, so the food was not destined to end in the kitchen.

What is the kitchen? If you look at it one way, it's a place of endless preparations, punctuated with periods of dealing with the aftermath, by which I mean the cleaning up. But we have to keep in mind *constantly* that the Christian faith sees such service as a form of exaltation. Faith that works in love, as the text above says, is not faith that seeks out the limelight. When we serve one another *in love*, we come to learn that God has designed the world to work in such a way that the majority of the time, we don't get the credit we think we deserve. Self can work hard, but it chafes under the biblical way of working hard. Love gives it away. And when everyone in the family loves—the kind of love you see in a Christian kitchen—the effect is glorious.

PRIORITIES

We are familiar with the story of Martha and Mary, and how Martha lost her sense of priorities because she was "cumbered about much serving."

> Now it came to pass, as they went, that he entered into a certain village: and a certain woman named Martha received him into her house. And she had a sister called Mary, which also sat at Jesus' feet, and heard his word. But Martha was cumbered about much serving, and came to him, and said, Lord, dost thou not care that my sister hath left me to serve alone? bid her therefore that she help me. And Jesus answered and said unto her, Martha, Martha, thou art careful and troubled about many things: But one thing is needful: and Mary hath chosen that good part, which shall not be taken away from her. (Lk. 10:38–42)

There are two applications here, and one of them very familiar. Unbroken fellowship with Christ is more important than having the meal turn out "just so." As noted in the last chapter, we will have frequent call to remember what Proverbs teaches us. "Better is a dry morsel, and quietness therewith, than an house full of sacrifices with strife" (Prov. 17:1).

But the other application is perhaps less familiar, and so it should perhaps receive more of our attention. Mary was listening to the Messiah teach; she was not off in the family room watching television or thumbing through her favorite magazines on the couch. She obviously knew some things were more important than serving in the kitchen. We may also be confident that she knew what Martha knew—that many other things are far *less* important than serving in the kitchen. "For as the body without the spirit is dead, so faith without works is dead also" (Jas. 2:26). So if a mother is harried in the kitchen because a number of her children are out in the living room being selfish, this is not a Mary and Martha situation at all. It's one where she will have to guard her attitude closely, but the children should not assume (when they are required to pitch in) that this is a case of misplaced priorities. Well, actually, it *is* a case of misplaced priorities—*theirs*.

BRICKS WITHOUT STRAW
One of the central duties husbands have is to make sure they don't exasperate their wives in this realm. Just as a woman is to work hard in preparing meals, so a man is to work hard in providing her with the food to work with. The Old Testament contains a relevant law concerning this which we will look at again later in this book. For now, it should simply be noted that provision of food was one of a man's central obligations. "If he take him another wife; her food, her raiment, and her duty of marriage, shall he not diminish" (Exod. 21:10).

This is not a commandment that says it's a sin to be poor. Rather, it addresses the husband's priorities. In other words, he cannot diminish his wife's allotment in these areas for the sake of a second wife. If he does so, then his refusal to care for a first wife for the sake of a second was grounds for divorce. Consequently this helps us to define what a monogamous man's responsibilities to his wife actually are in the first place.

One of them has to do with the state of her cupboards—he is to make sure she has enough food to work with. It is particularly important there be no disconnect in his mind between his failure to provide and his discontent with the culinary results. Too often men complain about the food in its cooked state because they are insensitive to their wives' concerns about food in its uncooked state. This is what a simpler era called bringing home the bacon. And if he doesn't bring it, she can't fry it.

OTHER PRIORITIES

As we work on conforming our lives more and more to Scripture, we will find that we have to make choices about what we should do first. What should be important to us?

First, a kitchen should be clean. We are going to look at the scriptural basis for saying this when we come to other parts of the house, but since we have come to the kitchen I need to simply assert something about this here. Cleanliness *is* next to godliness, and this has important ramifications for the kitchen. A kitchen should be clean and functional first and decorated (like in the magazines) second. This is not bare utilitarianism—the second aspect should be there. A kitchen is far more than a food laboratory, but it should be as clean as a laboratory.

As the food comes out of the kitchen, presentation is important and is part of what every accomplished cook should be concerned with. The ceremonial is far more than just ceremonial. At the same time, the ceremonial should not take over—beware of those who have the form of religion but not the substance. The presentation of food should be an aesthetic accomplishment, but beware of art food that photographs quite well yet requires three glasses of milk to get down.

The kitchen should not be a place where boys and men are aliens. Any masculinity that washes off in dishwater had to have been pretty superficial to begin with. The one place in the Bible that mentions dishwashing, interestingly, doesn't mention women. "And I will stretch over Jerusalem the line of Samaria, and the plummet of the house of Ahab: and I will wipe Jerusalem as a man wipeth a dish, wiping it, and turning it upside down" (2 Kgs. 21:13).

At the same time, it's important for us to have and

maintain our roles in the keeping of the house. We should reject the modern egalitarian nonsense that obliterates the different roles of men and women. As we have already discussed, women have a central role in running the operations of the home, and this includes the preparations of the kitchen. But once this is said, we need to remember that part of the reason for the distinction is that it makes gift-giving possible. In other words, different roles should never obscure the fact that both sides are living sacrificially—*my life for yours*. And sometimes that means crossover help.

All this said, we return to the centrality of charity. We return to the importance of serving one another in love. We return to the glory of service in obscurity.

CHAPTER SIX

Unwanted Guests: Bitterness

And when they came to Marah, they could not drink of the waters of Marah, for they were bitter: therefore the name of it was called Marah. And the people murmured against Moses, saying, What shall we drink? And he cried unto the LORD; and the LORD shewed him a tree, which when he had cast into the waters, the waters were made sweet: there he made for them a statute and an ordinance, and there he proved them, And said, If thou wilt diligently hearken to the voice of the LORD thy God, and wilt do that which is right in his sight, and wilt give ear to his commandments, and keep all his statutes, I will put none of these diseases upon thee, which I have brought upon the Egyptians: for I am the LORD that healeth thee. And they came to Elim, where were twelve wells of water, and three-score and ten palm trees: and they encamped there by the waters. (Exod. 15:23–27)

Bitterness is a sin which tempts us to be distracted, and this keeps us from looking where God's Word requires us to look. Because bitterness has deceived many, it's our responsibility to pray that the God of heaven would teach us to be wise about this great evil. It's a sin which has destroyed countless marriages and families. It's often tolerated for years after it first becomes a visible fixture in the household.

The people of Israel in their wanderings came to a hard circumstance. The waters of Marah were bitter waters, which the people could not drink. Because of this, the people began to murmur and grumble; *they* became bitter, just like the water. This is how bitterness in the form of trial often becomes bitterness in the form of rebellion. Moses prayed to the Lord who showed him a tree that would make the waters sweet when thrown into the water. He did so, and immediately after this, Moses made a statute and ordinance with the people, casting a comparable tree into their midst. This is the tree that must be thrown into your water. Diligently listen to the Lord; do what is right according to Him; listen to His commandments and keep His statutes. Then the Lord will keep them free of the diseases of Egypt; God will heal them, just as He healed the waters. And they came to Elim, where there were twelve wells of good water and seventy palm trees.

Of course, there is a righteous bitterness. We must not become superstitious about words. We have seen that the Bible prohibits certain forms of anger (Eph. 4:31), for example, and requires others (Eph. 4:26). It's the same kind of thing with bitterness. We are addressing the *sin* of bitterness here, but we must also remember the entire scope of God's Word to us. There is a bitterness in repentance, for example. "And Peter went out, and wept *bitterly*" (Lk. 22:62). And there is the hard providence that drives us to rely upon the Lord, as Hannah did. "And she was in *bitterness* of soul, and prayed unto the LORD, and wept sore" (1 Sam. 1:10; cf., Ruth 1:20–21). But we must also be careful; we might sin even here when a hard providence doesn't drive us to the Lord.

When we sin by falling into bitterness, we are sinning against others. The fact that these "others" may have started it doesn't keep us from sinning against them through bitterness. And when others sin against us, we often forget that God is behind it. As the Puritan Thomas Watson noted, we know all about the one who *brought* this trial to us and forget the one who *sent* it. When we stumble in this way, we are disobeying the Word of God to us. And how can we complain when others disobey the Word when we do the same thing? There are two key passages we must consider. The first gives the flat prohibition.

> And grieve not the holy Spirit of God, whereby ye are sealed unto the day of redemption. *Let all bitterness*, and wrath, and anger, and clamour, and evil speaking, *be put away from you*, with all malice. (Eph. 4:30–31)

Bitterness is simply inconsistent with how God intends for His people to live. The second passage illustrates the consequences of disobedience.

> Follow peace with all men, and holiness, without which no man shall see the Lord: Looking diligently lest any man fail of the grace of God; lest any root of bitterness springing up trouble you, and thereby many be defiled. (Heb. 12:14–15)

Bitterness is a root, and roots seek out something to feed on. As they feed, they grow, and when this plant comes to the surface, many are defiled. If I do something wrong, whenever I think about it, what comes to mind is *my* wrong. But what if someone does something wrong to me and I become bitter? Whenever I think about it, what comes to mind is what was done to me and not my own bitterness. If I tell a lie, then of course I have to correct it. But if someone lies *about* me, and spreads it all over town, the strong temptation is to focus on *their* lie and not on my *own* resentment. But I can confess the sins of other people all day long, and my joy in the Lord is not restored.

The Scriptures give us different descriptions of how bitterness can originate.

One is the sin of worshipping another god—turning from God leads to sin, and sin leads to bitterness (Deut. 32:31–33; Jer. 2:19; 4:17–18). This is bitterness that strikes at the heart. Another cause is greed and envy. When Simon saw the power that was with Peter, he tried to get it by means of his god, which was money (Acts 8:18–23). Peter identified him as a slave of bitterness. Third, bitterness is a consequence of sweet sin—sin that seemed like a good idea at the time (Prov. 5:3–4). Sexual entanglements often lead to great bitterness. And a fourth occasion of bitterness is right here at home—*intimate tangles*. Paul had obviously had some pastoral experience with this: "Husbands, love your wives, and be not bitter against them" (Col. 3:19).

YOU KNOW YOU ARE BITTER WHEN . . .

There are some telltale signs that would be good for every member of the household to be aware of.

Bitterness always has a sharp memory *for all the details*. And this is because bitterness has good study habits: review, review, review.

It's also true that bitterness frequently resorts to *anonymous critiques or attacks*. Bitter words are frequently unsigned. This is obviously more difficult to accomplish inside a home, but sin can be pretty creative.

> Hide me from *the secret counsel* of the wicked; from the insurrection of the workers of iniquity: Who whet their tongue like a sword, and bend their bows to shoot their arrows, *even bitter words*: That they may *shoot in secret* at the perfect: suddenly do they shoot at him, and fear not. (Ps. 64:2–4)

Another good indicator is the practice of conducting imaginary conversations in the mind. "*Then* I says to him, I says . . ." And of course, during these imaginary conversations, the brunt of this   brilliant repartee is never capable of coming back with anything intelligible at all.

Bitterness also starts to invert the moral order of things.

> Woe unto them that call evil good, and good evil; that put darkness for light, and light for darkness; that put bitter for sweet, and sweet for bitter." (Is. 5:20)

A bitter person frequently starts to approve what they would have never approved at an earlier time in their life. When a Christian finds himself justifying what he would never have approved in other circumstances, he is probably bitter.

As we saw earlier in the passage from Hebrews 12, bitterness is like a root. It grows. It gathers nutrients everywhere it can. Soon the person's heart and mouth are *full of it*—"Whose mouth is full of cursing and bitterness" (Rom. 3:14). What happens when the jar of your life is jostled? What comes out? If bitterness splashes on to everyone, this simply tells us what the jar was already full of.

A husband or wife(or child) who is convicted by the Spirit of God over his embrace of that great destroyer bitterness needs to make simple application. He must confess his own sin (1 Jn. 1:9) *as though he was the only one at fault.* On paper, he knows this is unlikely, and theologically he may know it's impossible, but for all practical purposes, bitterness doesn't know how to think about the faults of others—and so should not do so at all.

What is the conclusion of all this? What kind of fountain are you in your home? What kind of water are you? Is your name Marah or Elim? James teaches us that it must be one way or the other.

> *Doth a fountain send forth at the same place sweet water and bitter?* Can the fig tree, my brethren, bear olive berries? either a vine, figs? so can no fountain both yield salt water and fresh. Who is a wise man and endued with knowledge among you? let him shew out of a good conversation his works with meekness of wisdom. *But if ye have bitter envying and strife in your hearts*, glory not, and lie not against the truth. (Jas. 3:11–14)

CHAPTER SEVEN

The Dining Room on the Sabbath

And the LORD *spake unto Moses, saying, Speak unto
the children of Israel, and say unto them, Concerning
the feasts of the* LORD, *which ye shall proclaim to be
holy convocations, even these are my feasts. Six days
shall work be done: but the seventh day is the sabbath
of rest, an holy convocation; ye shall do no work
therein: it is the sabbath of the* LORD *in all your dwell-
ings.* (Lev. 23:1–3)

We now come to the dining room, with our first consideration being the observation of the Lord's Day as it relates
to dining. This is because how we honor God (or not) in an
overt way drives or defines how we honor Him (or not) in
our day-to-day activity as we are dealing with the other
members of the family. We are to love God, and *therefore*
we are to love our neighbor.

The creation of a new heaven and new earth necessi-
tated the establishment of a new sabbath to accompany it.
Just as God created the world in six days and nights and
then rested on the seventh day, so Christ *re*created the
world in three days and nights and rose again on the first
day (Heb. 4:9–10). This is why a sabbath rest remains
for us as the people of God. Since the first century, Christians have been marking this day as special, the Lord's
Day (Rev. 1:10), and have feasted on this weekly Easter
(Acts 20:7; 1 Cor. 16:2).

The text cited above shows us that the Old Testament

sabbath was intended as a *feast*, not a *fast*. But the same thing carries over into the New Testament as well. And it has to be said that wrong-headed obedience to this command has resulted in sabbatarian fasting, *which is a form of sabbath breaking*. The Lord's Day is not a penitential season. Paul tells the Corinthians they are to keep the *feast* while getting rid of the yeast of malice and wickedness (1 Cor. 5:7–8). Jude tells his readers that the presence of false teachers was a blemish in their *feasting* (Jude 11–12). Among other things, this assumes that Christians are called to feast on the Lord's Day. This necessarily involves kitchens and dining rooms.

DEATH AND RESURRECTION

We know that we worship in church because Jesus died on the cross and rose again from the dead. We know that we are forgiven for all our sins for the same reason. But we often don't recognize how deeply this gospel truth is imbedded in the world. Consider the dining room table set and ready for dinner. Virtually every type of food on the table is there for our life and has died for our life. The only exceptions I can think of would be the salt, the ice cubes, and the water. In other words, all food was once alive and was killed so that we might continue to live. Because we have allowed ourselves to become disconnected from the entire process, we tend to think of food as simple generic "food" and not as life surrendered.

This confusion is an easy one. When they were all very little, one of our children asked his mother if farmers grew their own food. When an affirmative answer was given, the question came back, "Don't they know how to cook?" But something called "food" doesn't mysteriously appear at the grocery store all shrink-wrapped—it grew, lived and died somewhere. And whenever we give thanks for food, we are thanking God *for the gospel*.

TASTE AND CEREMONY

God most emphatically is not a utilitarian. He could have devised a world in which nutritious food was available by the ton, like so much tasteless bran mash in a trough. We could easily have been kept alive with food that tasted uniformly like stewed hay. But what has God in fact done? He has made a big deal out of this process by doing a *lot* of unnecessary stuff. If we just begin to catalog what God thinks of food, we are instantly overwhelmed, just on the basis of how it *tastes*. Just think of butter, oranges, milk, watermelon, garlic, salt, wine, steak, potatoes, bacon, and grapes.

Now what do we do? Of course we appreciate this with gratitude but then as obedient children *we are to imitate*. And we imitate by doing "unnecessary" things in the cooking, in the setting of the table, and in the eating. These unnecessary things have to be more than *just* unnecessary—hassles are frequently unnecessary too—they also have to be pleasant like the taste of a tangerine. And because we are considering here the sabbath as feast, the cooking should be a cut above, the table set more nicely, and the manners more pleasant. In short, imitate God in the preparing of a special sauce, in placing flowers on the table, and in serving others at the table in love.

ATTITUDES

And this brings us to the matter of sabbath attitudes. A great danger with subjects like this one is that we all have a tendency to the sidelong glance. In other words, we wonder why *others* in the family are not doing *their* part. Or the sidelong glance is an envious one—*other* families are enjoying what we don't have a chance to enjoy. But remember, each family has its own gifts, personality, and capacity for blessing—its own unique way to glorify God. This may not be happening—in other words, families *can* fail in what they ought to be doing—but this is *not* because one family is not a mirror image of some other family. Feel free to copy *tips*, but don't fall for the trap of envying gifts. In this, remember that the sabbath is not raw demand. It is rest, glory, and peace. The Holy Spirit here works by seduction. The Lord's Day celebration around a table is altogether lovely.

PRACTICAL APPLICATIONS

The suggestions that follow are not intended as a voice from Sinai. We don't want to be legalistic in how we impose details on one another. At the same time, we don't want to leave families out if they are eager to apply these things but don't have any practical notion of how to proceed. So, if such suggestions for sabbath celebration are helpful to you, then wonderful. If not, then feel free to head in a different direction just so long as it's equally glad.

In starting the Lord's Day celebration, *start at the shallow end.* Don't try to do everything or learn everything all at once. That's the way to discouragement. If someone wants to begin jogging, they should not try ten miles on the first day. That's a good way to do nothing on the second day. Simply set your sabbath dinner apart, no matter how modest you think the distinction is.

Many families in our church observe the Lord's Day from 6 pm Saturday to 6 pm Sunday. The first century Jews did something similar to this—sundown to sundown. The point is not to reenact a scrupulous historical accuracy, but rather to choose of pattern of honoring the Lord's Day. Many conscientious Christians follow the Roman system of marking days, which is midnight to midnight. When it comes down to it, as a matter of measuring spirituality, who cares?

But, at the same time, there is a real practical advantage that attends celebration that moves from 6 to 6. This pattern means the cook can do the bulk of the work on Saturday and sit down to enjoy the beginning of the sabbath with the rest of the family. The work and cooking is still being done at 5:45, and yet the cook can begin resting with the family at 6, and the food is still hot. And if it's a real good business, you have great leftovers to enjoy after worship on Sunday. The one downside is that you can find yourself mixing Jewish and Roman ways of counting the hours, and so you begin the celebration Saturday, asking for the Lord to bless our worship of Him on the Lord's Day *tomorrow*. But you can't have everything.

We need to come to understand the nature of blessing. And we have to emphasize, this is not for rich people. All families, at whatever level they live, know how to enjoy their "best." So this is simply a question of priorities—save your best, whatever it is, for the Lord's Day. This includes the best wine, the best chocolate, the best dishes, etc. If treats are few and far between, place them here in order to honor God, in order to bless His name.

The Lord's Day is marked off with the Word of God. So as we honor the Lord's Day, we don't do so as mimes. We are to *speak* about these things both to the Lord and to one another. Here is a suggested simple ceremony—special "manners" for the sabbath to be woven in with your regular practices. But as said before, just follow this pattern if it's helpful.

First, welcome all visitors to your table. Second, offer a prayer of thanks which includes particular recognition of the sabbath. Third, the little children can answer their catechism questions. Q. What day is it? A. It is the Lord's Day. Q. Why is it the Lord's Day? A. Because Jesus rose from the dead. Q. What kind of day is it? A. It is a sweet day. Then you can all sing a psalm together, and the dinner begins. Singing during clean up is another great blessing.

CHAPTER EIGHT

The Dining Room

Now the Spirit speaketh expressly, that in the latter times some shall depart from the faith, giving heed to seducing spirits, and doctrines of devils; Speaking lies in hypocrisy; having their conscience seared with a hot iron; Forbidding to marry, and commanding to abstain from meats, which God hath created to be received with thanksgiving of them which believe and know the truth. For every creature of God is good, and nothing to be refused, if it be received with thanksgiving: For it is sanctified by the word of God and prayer.
(1 Tim. 4:1–5)

Viewed by a reductionist, eating is a mere biological necessity, the organic equivalent of putting fuel in the car. And of course, if we ever saw someone carrying on at the gas station the way we carry on in the dining room, we would want to have them committed. But unfortunately, this ridiculous example is actually working the other way—far too many of us treating the dining room as a mere filling station.

What sort of thing would devils teach if given the opportunity? What would they say if given the pulpit next Sunday? What would a seducing spirit say if given the chance to sear the conscience of a Bible teacher with a hot iron?

At the very top of the list would be prohibitions of food and sex. But for those who believe and who know the truth, such things were created by God in order to be received *with thanksgiving*. This means gratitude, gladness, and contentment. If God made it, there is a good use for it, and frequently this good use includes having been sauteed in butter. The word of God and prayer sanctifies all creatures, including the creatures *on* the table for those creatures *around* the table.

IDOLATRY AND FOOD

We have to begin by guarding ourselves against error. We are a fallen race, and John's admonition to keep ourselves from idols has to be constantly kept in mind (1 Jn. 5:21). This is particularly true for Americans, who have a long tradition of locating righteousness and unrighteousness in their food and drink. The locations change, but the basic orientation does not. But Jesus taught us a man cannot be spiritually defiled by what goes into his mouth (Mk. 7:18–19).

We can check our hearts in this by the presence or absence of religious indignation over "violations." If someone reacts to fast food like an orthodox rabbi watching someone frying bacon, then he is a food idolater. If you are watching what you eat for simple health reasons, then this is not the case. But we even have to be careful here, because health is another great American idol.

Carrie Nation attacked demon rum. John Harvey Kellogg invented corn flakes as breakfast food without meat—designed to reduce the sexual drive. Reducing bestial animal desire through food was the order of the day, and it was even thought you could pass on less original sin to your kids this way. Sylvester Graham invented Graham flour for this purpose, a shield against vile affections. We see in the development of s'mores a triumph of trinitarian practice over cultic ideology. Despite this triumph, Americans are still culturally predisposed to believe one can be "put right," whatever that means, through whatever is put in the mouth.

And when this sort of health fascist gets into the church,

one of the first things he finds is that verse in Corinthians about the body being the Temple of the Holy Spirit. But note what Paul actually says.

> Flee fornication. Every sin that a man doeth is without the body; but he that committeth fornication sinneth against his own body. What? know ye not that your body is the temple of the Holy Ghost which is in you, which ye have of God, and ye are not your own? For ye are bought with a price: therefore glorify God in your body, and in your spirit, which are God's. (1 Cor. 6:18–20)

All other sins are "outside the body," but sexual sin is against the body. This means that such things as smoking tobacco and eating mounds of refined sugar can perhaps be argued against as forms of poor stewardship, but such "sins" are not against the body. The temple of the Holy Spirit can be desecrated by fornication, but it's not desecrated by hardening the arteries thereof. The physical act of eating does not have the spiritual import that American health cultists have attributed to it. Eating *is* profoundly spiritual, and that is actually the point of this chapter. But spirituality is *not* what they have construed it to be. True spirituality involves ice cream, particularly if you have the kind of fudge sauce my wife makes.

So gluttony is not about that second helping of mashed potatoes at Thanksgiving. At the same time, the issues here remain important ones. Gluttony does *not* refer to a desire to eat and drink, but rather to an inordinate desire. But when we use words like *inordinate*, we have to remember to ask the fundamental question—by what standard?

In the same section as our earlier passage, we read this: "Know ye not that the unrighteous shall not inherit the kingdom of God? . . . Meats for the belly, and the belly for meats: but God shall destroy both it and them" (1 Cor. 6:9,13). We are to worship God with our stomachs without worshipping our stomachs. We do this remembering that God will translate our whole created order to another level. The fact that this resurrection level will not be gaseous and ethereal does not change the fact that in the resurrection the belly will be swallowed up in life. What the heck does that mean? Unfortunately, the glutton will never know.

We are to identify gluttony by the company it keeps. The sin condemned in Scripture as gluttony is identified by its companions. The word is *zalal*, and refers to riotous eating. As such, gluttony exasperates parents. In the book of Deuteronomy, we see what happens when parents of a glutton bring him in. "And they shall say unto the elders of his city, This our son is stubborn and rebellious, he will not obey our voice; he is a glutton, and a drunkard" (Deut. 21:20). As we see in the next verse, this sin warranted the death penalty—this was not a case of having an extra candy bar. The son in question was guilty of riotous and dissolute living.

We can also identify it by the end result. A glutton will come to poverty. "Hear thou, my son, and be wise, and guide thine heart in the way. Be not among winebibbers; among riotous eaters of flesh: for the drunkard and the glutton shall come to poverty: and drowsiness shall clothe a man with rags" (Prov. 23:19–21). This was the sin of the prodigal son (Lk. 15:13). He ran off and wasted his father's substance in riotous living.

Sins are like grapes—they come in bunches. Gluttony is necessarily related to other forms of sinful behavior. "Whoso keepeth the law is a wise son: but he that is a companion of riotous men shameth his father" (Prov. 28:7). It's bad enough even to be *associated* with people like this.

FATNESS AND GOOD CHEER

To keep our balance, we have to remember what the Bible says about fat.

The Bible uses the image of *fat* very differently than do we. In fact, in Scripture, leaving aside the fat of the sacrificial offerings, there are two basic connotations of fatness. One is that of insolence and rebellion (Ps. 17:10; 73:7; 119:70; Is. 6:10; Jer. 5:28; Job 15:27). Their eyes are like grease, so when we think of fat, we should think of Eglon and tyranny (Judg. 3:17).

But the other—somewhat surprising to natives of this fat-free culture—is that of abundant blessing (Gen. 27:28; 45:18; 49:20; Num. 13:20; Deut. 31:20; 1 Chr. 4:40; Ps. 22:29; 36:8; 65:11; 92:12–14; Prov. 11:25; 13:4; 28:25; Is. 10:16; 25:6; 55:2; 58:11). Fat is a wonderful blessing, and so when we think of it, we should also think of God's wonderful grace. "And they took strong cities, and a fat land, and possessed houses full of all goods, wells digged, vineyards, and oliveyards, and fruit trees in abundance: so they did eat, and were filled, *and became fat*, and delighted themselves in thy great goodness" (Neh. 9:25; cf., 8:10; 9:35). Clearly our standard cannot be the modern loathing of fat in every form. We need to do something about our milk that looks like water someone cleaned a paintbrush in.

This relates to our problem with "gluttony in reverse." We have already noted the fat-phobia of our culture. There is a spiritual danger here. A glutton is a belly-god. "For they that are such serve not our Lord Jesus Christ, but their own belly." (Rom. 16:18; cf., Phil. 3:18–19). But this is not successfully checked by any kind of asceticism. These are the commandments and doctrines of men, but are of no value in restraining the flesh (Col. 2:20–23). Americans have a deep faith in salvation through food. Either that, or no food. But Jesus taught that foodstuffs cannot defile a man (Mt. 15:17). The issue is self-control. Godly self-discipline is a result of the Spirit's work in our lives.

As Christians, we are to enjoy our food in the light of eternity, but we are not against practical considerations. If someone wants to lose weight for practical reasons—be able to tie his own shoes, that sort thing—then self-control should be encouraged. But this is difficult if our assumptions about eating are all wrong.

The sin of gluttony is therefore twofold. One is a lack of self-control with food—compulsive, driven behavior with food. The other is a finicky compulsion over food. The solution to either is not a new resolve to set up a new menu for yourself. The solution is to learn how to sit down at Christ's table. He has provided the fare, the bread and the wine.

THE NOBILITY OF DINING

As mentioned earlier, eating can be viewed (by the dull materialist) as simple fueling. His pedestrian mind thinks of chewing, swallowing, enzymes, gas, esophagi, and colons. But the human race is created in the image of God, and this means that eating is overwhelmingly treated as a ceremonial activity. This ceremony, this liturgy, these manners, *are not any less real* than the biological realities gathered around the table. The manners may differ from culture to culture, just as the sauces do, but the presence of them is nearly universal. In our casual era, with our ongoing revolt against giving honor to one another, this is something we must emphasize.

The way we emphasize it is through the inculcation of manners, which are simply the liturgy of dining. Such manners are a godly exhibition of love in trifles. Manners help us learn how to be considerate of one another—where everyone knows what is expected and thus knows *how* to give to others. But as manners are taught to the children, it's important to guard against certain pitfalls.

When it rains it pours, and so we have to guard against what might be called *rabbinical excesses*. We live in suburban America, and not in the court of Louis XIV. A mania for manners is in itself discourteous to others. So parents should take care not become overzealous nutcases. Manners are designed to adorn and beautify our lives, not to gum them up. This is why we must not *forget the point*—manners are to be a help for us as we seek to enjoy one another at the table. Forgetting the point can be seen in harsh correction of a violation. Fundamental rudeness in correcting incidental rudeness is a common problem. Let's say that a twelve-year-old boy licked his knife, which is, as they say, not done in the better circles. But let's also try to imagine something which is not that hard, which is one of his parents climbing down his throat for it. In correcting manners, *remember your manners*.

TABLE TALK
The practice of sharing bread together is what gave our word *companion*. In a very important sense, the *way* we spend time at the table as a family actually amounts to a *second meal*. It is a familial *koinonia*, or fellowship, and results in true companionship. If your thousands of shared meals don't result in companionship, then something is seriously wrong.

The moderator sits at the head of the table. The husband and father has important responsibilities here, but his gifts and his office should not be confused. He doesn't have to be the talkative one, but he is there to maintain order. The head of the table moderates. He has to talk enough to have his presence be supportive of the flow and direction of the conversation. He sees to it that everyone takes turns. Everyone eats, so why shouldn't everyone talk? But not all at once.

In this regard, we would do well to pay attention to the *one anothers* of Scripture. These "one anothers" are really quite striking. One of the best places to practice them in the home is at the table. We show affection and honor to one another here (Rom. 12:10); we love one another (Rom. 13:8); refuse to judge one another (Rom. 14:13); receive one another (Rom. 15:7); admonish one other (Rom. 15:14) and many others such things we do. This is how sharing food creates true companions.

CHAPTER NINE

Unwanted Guests: Anger

*And grieve not the holy Spirit of God, whereby ye are
sealed unto the day of redemption. Let all bitterness,
and wrath, and anger, and clamour, and evil speaking, be put away from you, with all malice: And be ye
kind one to another, tenderhearted, forgiving one another, even as God for Christ's sake hath forgiven you.*
(Eph. 4:30–32)

As we have known for centuries, anger is a brief madness.
And when a man comes to his senses again, after a fit of
anger, he has plenty of leisure to repent of the damage he
has done. But repairing the damage is often far more difficult than the mere desire to repair it.

Anger is one of the most destructive forces that can be
unleashed in a home. Unfortunately, this does not keep it
from being unleashed—even in many Christian homes. But
unless we have some biblical idea of what godly anger looks
like, we will have no way to repent of our ungodly anger.

We know from Scripture that Jesus got angry. When
He was presented with the man with a withered hand
as a trap, His response was one of anger and grief together
(Mk. 3:5). The Bible never tells us He was angry when He
cleansed the Temple (Mk. 11:15–17), although He probably was. In the passage, consider three things about His
righteous anger—the occasion for it, what accompanied it,
and the results of it. The thing that provoked His anger
was hardness of heart. Grief accompanied his anger, not a

red hot malicious rage. And last, consider that when Jesus got angry, the end result was a man with a healed hand. The result of ungodly anger is frequently a man with an injured hand because he tried to punch a hole in the wall.

We must also remember the anger of God. A great deal of what we see around us every day makes God angry. When a man remains in unbelief, the wrath of God abides on him (Jn. 3:36). This provides us with another important doctrinal category that prevents us from saying that anger *per se* is a sin.

Further, we are commanded to get angry. Be angry, the Bible commands us, but do not sin (Eph. 4:26). This is an imperative, a command. But, curious to note, this is just a few verses before our earlier text where we are told to put away *all* wrath and anger. So even if the anger is *righteous*, like manna, it will not keep overnight. So when we obey the command to be angry in a righteous way, we have to follow the pattern outlined for it in Scripture.

Part of this is remembering the judicial nature of anger in Scripture as justice is executed. Consider the flow of argument between Romans 12:19 and 13:6. Do not avenge yourselves, we are told (12:19), *but leave room for wrath.* But who is the agent of such wrath? The magistrate is God's deacon in this (13:4). This is why we avoid personal vengeance while feeling free to call the police.

Having noted all this, our most common problem is not one of how to deal with righteous anger. We have to deal with outbursts of temper—outburts for no good reason. Too many parents have devastated their children through such fits of anger. As with other sins, this one keeps bad company as well. It's one of the works of the flesh (Gal. 5:20). People whose lives are characterized by this do not inherit the kingdom (v. 21). Displays of rage and temper in a Christian home are the moral equivalent of keeping copies of *Penthouse* on the coffee table or bringing home shoplifted goods to show the family at dinner. People whose lives are characterized by this do not go to heaven.

Frequently, the children don't go there as well because they abandon the faith their hypocritical parents taught them, and they do so the first chance they get.

Paul says we are to put our wrath and anger away. We are also told to put it *off* (Col. 3:8). We are not our own; we were bought by someone else. He has told us to get the anger out of our lives, and this is because we have put on Christ.

In submitting to this, we are to have no patience with excuses. Note that the text is speaking to all followers of Christ—put it away. It does not say put it away *if*. . . . One may think he is not young enough to change, the provocations are too big for him to change, and so forth. But the word must be bluntly spoken to every follower of Christ—knock it off.

When we give way to anger, we are getting underfoot. God has a design for the Christian family, and unrighteous anger works to frustrate that design. The wrath of man worketh not the righteousness of God (Jas. 1:20). This means, among other things, that the anger interferes with a biblical solution with whatever it is that causes the anger. The parent who is angry complicates the problems of the home enormously.

In our lives together, we must note that anger frequently grows up from what we think are lesser sins—annoyances, irritations, resentments, gripes, imputations of motive, and so forth. An important part of dealing with the sin of anger is learning to recognize the storm when it's a small cloud. The way to be able to do this is to cultivate a tender heart. What is the counterpart to every form of anger? It is kindness, tenderheartedness, forgiveness to one another. This is the only measuring rod we may use.

In order to be genuinely freed from our own fits of anger and rage, we must contemplate through faith the greatest display of wrath in the history of the world—which was the cross of Jesus Christ. There, in the wrath of God, the petty wrath of all His people was crucified. The solution to *our* anger is not *our* lack of anger. The solution to our fits of anger is God's wrath with that anger.

> Much more then . . . we shall be saved from wrath through him. For if, when we were enemies, we were reconciled to God by the death of his Son, much more, being reconciled, we shall be saved by his life. (Rom. 5:9–10)

So we were saved *from* wrath *by* wrath. And if we have no glimpse of true wrath, we will spend our lives face down in the puddles of our own private animosities. Still less will we try to drown our children in them. Dear God, deliver us! But deliverance is only through the cross. An angry man will only be delivered from anger by seeing how angry God was with it. And that is seen when we look to the cross.

CHAPTER TEN

The Bedroom

Let brotherly love continue. Be not forgetful to enter-
tain strangers: for thereby some have entertained an-
gels unawares. Remember them that are in bonds, as
bound with them; and them which suffer adversity, as
being yourselves also in the body. Marriage is
honourable in all, and the bed undefiled: but
whoremongers and adulterers God will judge. Let your
conversation be without covetousness; and be content
with such things as ye have: for he hath said, I will
never leave thee, nor forsake thee. (Heb. 13:1–5)

One of our tasks as Christians is to bring everything we do
into conformity with the Scriptures, in every room of the
house. This obviously includes the bedroom (Rom. 12:1–2),
and, within that bedroom, the marriage bed.

This passage begins with an exhortation to brotherly
love, which sets the context for what follows (Heb. 13:1).
This love will result in hospitality, the entertaining of strangers (13:2). The next is the visiting of those who cannot
visit you. They may be in the hospital, bedridden at home,
or in prison (13:3). Paul then goes on to say that marriage
is honorable in all, and the bed undefiled (13:4). God judges
all infidelity and sexual corruptions. The root from which
this infidelity springs is a life of covetousness, a lack of contentment (13:5). But God has promised never to desert us,
and so there is no reason for that discontent.

Now as we work our way through the house, the rou-
tine applications are made to those who are married with

children. The reasons for this are obvious, but it's hope-
fully just as obvious that there are some erroneous and harm-
ful applications that could be drawn from this. Those who
are unmarried in the church ought never to be made to feel
like lepers, whether their single state is intentional or provi-
dential.

In a context where most adults are married, and in the
context of a church where marriage and family are emphasized and a cause of much rejoicing, it might be easy for the
unmarried to drift into a "fifth wheel" or "what's the use?"
mindset. The two rooms of the house where such problems are likely to be accentuated for the unmarried are the
dining room and the bedroom—and the problems can range
from self-pity to loneliness to laziness. But the unmarried
are called to establish healthy households, no less than those
who are married. The challenges are different, but the goal
of glorifying God remains the same. Being unmarried is no
legitimate barrier to obedience.

With regard to the bedroom, the unmarried honor the
marriage bed as much as do the married, but they do so by
different means. The first means is by honoring the vows
of *others*; an unmarried person can certainly commit adultery or fornication. Not everyone who defiles a marriage
bed is married. The second means is by cultivating a spirit
of contentment with what God has given (v. 5) for as long
as He chooses to give it. A discontent and chafing spirit
over the single state is a good way to wind up discontent
and unhappy in the married state.

At the same time, those who are married need to take
care that they don't adopt a patronizing attitude toward
households with an unmarried head. Lydia was as much the
head of her house as the Philippian jailer was (Acts 16:15).
Married folk need to be particularly careful about stray
comments; for example, "Why aren't you married yet?"
Also be careful about lowering the standards of civil behavior; don't make excuses of the sort that might help create a
two-tier system of families. Those who are unmarried are not
second-class citizens.

AND WHY ONE?

All this said, the normal pattern is that of marriage. God created mankind in His image, male and female created He them (Gen. 1:27). The fact that this design feature of sexuality has a large aesthetic element in it does not mean that it is aesthetic or recreational in isolation. In this, as in so many other areas of life, form follows function, and God has made the world in such a way that the form and function are complementary. The prophet Malachi asked why God had made man and woman.

> Yet ye say, Wherefore? Because the LORD hath been witness between thee and the wife of thy youth, against whom thou hast dealt treacherously: yet is she thy companion, and the wife of thy covenant. And *did not he make one?* Yet had he the residue of the spirit. And *wherefore* one? That he might seek *a godly seed.* Therefore take heed to your spirit, and let none deal treacherously against the wife of his youth. (Mal. 2:14–15)

Sexual relations have as one of their purposes the propagation of children. But there is a way of applying this purpose disobediently. Therefore take heed to the spirit. Such relations are not *merely* for the propagation of children but rather for the obtaining of a *godly* seed. Godly children don't grow up automatically simply because the parents have convictions against birth control. And the embrace of this *telos* of the marriage relation certainly does not exclude the other purposes God has bestowed on righteous sexual activity—from pleasure to companionship, from companionship and comfort to the preservation of purity. At the same time, the result of godly children remains something which should not be forgotten.

EROTIC OBEDIENCE

One of the ways to honor the marriage bed is to actually spend some time thinking about the *bed*, and about its surroundings. This should be obvious; all of us have spent about a third of our lives in some bed or another. One of the things we learn in the Song of Solomon is the importance of surroundings and context. The rafters are made of cedar.

There are two important points here. One is that a married couple should design and/or decorate the bedroom as though they were not highly spiritual gnostics or mundane pragmatists. The bed should not just be a place to dump the laundry. One of the ways to honor the marriage bed is to *make* that bed in the morning. The room should not be a chaotic jumble. When this happens, a negative "architectural" statement is being made, and the statement is that whatever goes on here is comparatively unimportant.

Of course, the marriage bed is honored as we keep the vows that we have made concerning it, but honor is not something that can be contained invisibly in the heart. What would we make of a man who was faithful to his wife sexually but who constantly belittled her? We could say he was honoring his vows in some sense, but in another important way, he was *not* honoring her. Honor must have an external rhetorical expression, whether in standing, saluting, or some other form of communicating. One way to honor the marriage bed in this way is to see that the sheets are changed regularly, the bed is made, and the bed and surrounding room are decorated appropriately. By this means a couple are saying they *esteem* what occurs there.

The second principle concerns the manner of honoring the bed privately in the way the couple treat one another sexually. The theme of "my life for yours," which is to permeate the rest of the house, should be pervasive here as well. There are few areas (I actually cannot think of any) where neglect of this principle has more devastating effects. Selfish grasping is a bad deal throughout the house, but in lovemaking, selfishness—where communion is designed to be the closest—creates a monstrous hypocrisy of the whole business and drives the couple farther apart than they could have imagined possible. If "my life for yours" does not govern in this realm, then sexual relations are made deadly and the font of all bitterness.

COMPANIONSHIP

When Adam first saw Eve, he wrote the first poem (Gen. 2:23). His bride was taken from his side in order to be given back to him. One became two in order that those two might become one again in another way, one that was far more delightful. We know that this partaking of one another is a type of the ultimate partaking, the *koinonia* in which the Lord and His people become one. As Paul noted, this was all a great mystery, but he was speaking of Christ and the Church. In some important sense, marriage, particularly in its sexual aspect, shows us in a figure something about the communion between the Lord and His people.

As this ultimate partaking is not a "mere" mechanical unity, neither is the type. Reductionist thinking in the one area will lead to reductionist thinking in the other. A low ecclesiology will lead necessarily to a low view of marriage. A low view of church membership vows will lead to a low view of marriage vows. In our day, when people walk away from local congregations so easily, why are we surprised when they do the same thing in their marriages? The sexual union is designed for closeness, fellowship, and companionship, and it's used by God to actually accomplish it. Our understanding of the erotic aspect of our lives will fill out our understanding of God's purpose for His people, and vice versa. But the apostle confessed that this whole thing was beyond him, and so I am not going to try to talk about it any further.

CHAPTER ELEVEN

Unwanted Guests: Lust

Mortify therefore your members which are upon the earth; fornication, uncleanness, inordinate affection, evil concupiscence, and covetousness, which is idolatry. (Col. 3:5)

We do not live in a time of public silence on lust. There has been no moratorium on the noise about it, the perpetual chatter that surrounds us on every side. Enticements to lust, discussions of lust, and inducements to lust are constant. Further, lust is a great threat to the unity and integrity of the Christian home. A marriage is a covenant with sexual union and fidelity at the center of it. Lust strikes at this, and the attacks, depending on the circumstances, can be both overt and subtle. Unfortunately, there is a great deal we have not yet learned about this.

One of the central things we have missed is the fact that God's Word on this comes to men and women both. The words above were written to the Colossian saints, not to the Colossian *men*. Yet, a very widespread assumption in the Christian world is that lust is a problem men have, while women deal with other temptations elsewhere. I have been providing pastoral marriage counseling for twenty-five years or more, and through that time, I have to say the number of unfaithful wives has been significantly greater than the number of unfaithful husbands. It's simply *not* true that women are not tempted in this area.

It *is* true that the avenue of temptation differs. Men

love to want, while women desire to be wanted. It's not as though men have a problem with lust and women don't. The two sexes actually have complementary problems with this sin. Just as our physiological makeup is complementary, so it is with our mental framework. Our respective temptations correspond with one another; they are concave and convex. When men look unlawfully, it's because they have this problem with lust. When women behave and dress to be looked *at*, they have this problem also. This is why the Bible tells women to be modest (1 Tim. 2:9).

But it's not quite so simple as this. *Before* it gets to the level of a woman seeking to attract a man's sexual attention, a great deal of preliminary work must be done. This is because (generally) men are first attracted to a woman physically and then emotionally. With women, this order is (generally) reversed. They first get involved emotionally and then physically. Once it gets to the physical level for them, a number of the things discussed below come into play.

Imagine a couple who are unhappy and have been for a number of years. Suppose they quarrel one morning, and he stomps off to go to work. Suppose further that on this day a woman at his work makes a pass of some sort. Provided she is attractive, he doesn't even need to know her name to be tempted. If he succumbs to the temptation, he *will* get emotionally involved, but that comes later.

Something comparable to this happening at home is extremely unlikely. His wife is as vulnerable to the temptations of adultery as he is but is unlikely to be tempted at all by an offer made by the washing machine repairman. Her temptations would come in another form. Let's say the husband next door took time to visit with her over the back fence, he got the lawn mower started for her once, and it seems like he's really interested in *listening* (unlike you know who). She is first tempted emotionally and then physically. Incidentally (or perhaps not so incidentally), this is why many adulterous relationships have happened in counseling situations—the counselor or pastor does all the things her husband *should* be doing—listening, providing guidance and empathy, and so on. And this is why wise counselors take wise preventative measures.

When things have deteriorated to a certain point, a woman can begin behaving provocatively in order to get a sexual response. This can happen when a woman is stubborn and loose (what used to be called *abandoned*), but it can also happen when a woman is emotionally desperate. In other words, she can behave in sexually provocative ways, not because of overt sexual lust, but rather because of an emotional lust, which is not detachable from sex however much we want to pretend.

However it happens, when it gets to this level, we can learn a great deal from Proverbs 7:1–23. What are some of the characteristics of this kind of provocation?

We are told the woman dresses in a way that communicates her sexual availability. She dresses like a prostitute (7:10). Obviously there are gradations of this, but they are gradations of the same problem. We need to take care here, because much of this modern hookerware has already been mainstreamed and is for sale at a department store near you. Moms—sometimes reluctantly, sometimes not—buy such clothes for their daughters. Sometimes older women buy them for themselves for various reasons ranging from mild insecurity to desperation. Whatever the reason, the clothing is objectively calculated to evoke a certain response. In the fashion industry, getting men to look is a *science*. And while Christian women have a responsibility to dress attractively, this is very different from dressing in order to attract.

The woman has a subtle, tangled heart. She is crafty, and knows how to set and bait the trap (7:10). Because of this subtle approach, she also has what is called deniability. This has become a marked feature of our schizophrenic society—women dressing in order to provoke a response but being able to deny this is what they were doing.

She is also stubborn and headstrong. When it's pointed out what she is doing, she doesn't have the frame of heart to hear it. She is brash, loud, and stubborn (Prov. 7:11). What is a daughter's response if mom says her jeans are too tight? What is a wife's response if her husband says he doesn't like how other men look at her when they are out? If it's a response of rolling the eyes, the problem is already there.

The tendency is to wander away from home; her feet don't like it at home. Home is *boring* (7:11). While away, she can be sexually aggressive. She is impudent, and she makes the proposition verbal (7:13). The proposition, however, has already been made by this point but just has not been spoken aloud. She makes lots of promises; she promises him a good time, as countless popular songs put it, "all night long" (7:18). In this context, she often uses flattery. Her words drip with honey; she knows how to use pseudo-respect (7:21).

It's hardly as though men are innocent bystanders, however. When a woman is in desperate straits, it's because a man put her there. And there is no shortage of men prepared to take full advantage of it. Men who want to stay faithful must remember that lust is not a sensation; it's a road with an established destination. That destination is always some form of sexual immorality. When lust is planted, the harvest is consistently some sort of sexual grief.

This is why men are told to flee or abstain. Paul tells Timothy to *flee* youthful lusts (2 Tim. 2:22). Peter tells us to abstain from fleshly lusts which war against the soul (1 Pet. 2:11). Whenever Potiphar's wife starts to unbutton her blouse, *run away*. It doesn't matter if it looks foolish to others. This means men should avoid women who dress immodestly, drastically alter the movies they watch, have nothing to do with porn on the net or late-night cable, and so forth. A man may believe he has no intent to abandon his wife and family, but giving way to this kind of behavior makes the statement that he is *thinking* about it. Allowing lust free rein in the mind is playing with gasoline and matches. Men must learn to consider the end; the young man in Proverbs did not think or anticipate the results of his behavior (Prov. 7:7,22–23).

The world teaches on this subject all the time. How many of these lessons have husbands mastered, and how much of the *Bible's* teaching on lust, sex, marriage, men, women, etc., have they studied? How can those who refuse to *learn* think to teach or lead?

The greatest earthly help to faithfulness, for both men and women, is the institution of marriage. The grace of God in this is not necessarily heavenly. We must set our minds on Christ, seated at the right hand of the Father, but in doing this, we heed His word. In His word, He tells us the marriage bed is to be *honored*; the author of Hebrews tells us this plainly (Heb. 13:4). This means sexual living is to be highly esteemed among Christians, but we don't esteem it highly if we ignore it. Prayers and blessings at Christian weddings ought to routinely refer to the marriage bed, and everyone there should know this public gathering is called for the purpose of celebrating a new sexual relationship, one that will begin later that day.

So the marriage bed is to be used. The world is filled with immorality, and the apostle Paul tells us that one of the functions of marriage in a fallen world is to help guard against temptations to immorality (1 Cor. 7:2–3). In this, the marriage bed is to be a delight: the godly man is commanded to be satisfied with his wife's breasts and is to be ravished with her love (Prov. 5:19). A couple should get drunk on one another (Song 5:1).

But as Christians, we must also go beyond earthly means. Under Christ, such things are helps but not ultimate solutions. As we have seen elsewhere, the solution is not new resolutions but rather *Christ*. The antidote to lust is not to extinguish desire but rather to direct it rightly. We must learn to love God, at whose right hand are pleasures forevermore (Ps. 16:11). When we give way to lust, it's not because our desire is inflamed; rather the desire of lust is pathetically anemic.

CHAPTER TWELVE

Sleep in the Bedroom

*My son, let not them depart from thine eyes: keep sound
wisdom and discretion: So shall they be life unto thy
soul, and grace to thy neck. Then shalt thou walk in
thy way safely, and thy foot shall not stumble. When
thou liest down, thou shalt not be afraid: yea, thou
shalt lie down, and thy sleep shall be sweet. Be not
afraid of sudden fear, neither of the desolation of the
wicked, when it cometh. For the* LORD *shall be thy
confidence, and shall keep thy foot from being taken.*
(Prov. 3:21–26)

Like marriage, work, and food, sleep existed before the fall
of mankind into sin. It is part of the creation order and is
one of those things God pronounced as good. Sin has af-
fected sleep, of course, as it has done with every other aspect of our being, but there is nevertheless something
foundationally *good* here, and an important part of our sanctification lies in learning to lie down and go to sleep. Discipleship extends even to this. We are to present our bodies
a living sacrifice (Rom. 12:1–2), and this means whatever
we are on is an altar: the seat of our car, the chair at the
office, and the bed where we lie. The chief end of man is to
glorify God and enjoy him forever, and this includes how
we live for this significant portion of our lives. I am fifty
years old as I write this, which means that I have spent
approximately sixteen of those years sound asleep. That's
sixteen times around the sun, and God apparently wants all

of us to spend roughly that percentage of our time conked out. How are we to honor Him as we do this?

SCRIPTURAL BACKGROUND ON SLEEP

Throughout the Scriptures, sleep is an important type for death. This includes creative death (that is, death followed by resurrection), and it includes death without hope. For the former, consider Adam at the formation of Eve (Gen. 2:21) or Abraham when God ratified the covenant with him (Gen. 15:12). For an example of the latter, consider sleep as a spiritual stupor and judgment (Is. 29:10). Throughout the Scriptures, sleep is also used as a metaphor for physical death (Deut. 31:16; 2 Sam. 7:12; 1 Thes. 4:14)

Sleep is a covenant blessing, one which the Scriptures describe as sweet (Prov. 3:24). Sleep is described as a fruit of wisdom. Sleep is also a snare for the lazy (Prov. 6:9–11). It is the state prior to conversion (Eph. 5:14). Elsewhere we see that sleep is a type for lethargy in the Church, calling for reformation (Rom. 13:11).

A CAUTION

We have to be careful in how we apply the Scriptures in all this. We should approach these things with caution and a willingness to learn, which is not the same thing as anxiety or panic. The last thing we want is someone with a sleep disorder concluding after they read this that they are in deep sin and are about to get a visit from the elders. *That* should help them doze off!

We have to take care not to fall into the fallacy called "affirming the consequent." Sin problems often *do* result in sleep problems, but this doesn't mean that all sleep problems are sin problems. Dogs have four legs, but this doesn't make a cow a dog. If a man cannot sleep because of the neighbor's dog endlessly barking, there may be a resultant spiritual problem, but that problem did not cause the sleep-lessness. Many times people cannot sleep because of noise, pain, excitement, and so on. There is obviously no spiritual problem with such things. But sleeplessness that is the re-sult of anxiety or frustration is a different matter. Sleepless-ness and sin are interrelated realities, but not automatically.

A DOOR ON ITS HINGES

One common sin related to sleep is called "getting too much of it" or getting it at inappropriate times. The Scriptures teach us plainly there is a high correlation between this kind of behavior and poverty. "Slothfulness casteth into a deep sleep; and an idle soul shall suffer hunger" (Prov. 19:15). Notice that sloth brings on deep sleep which can be thought of as a deep curse. Someone can be dead to the world because they work very hard, but the Bible teaches that they can also be dead to the world because they don't work at all. One of the great ways we can honor the Lord for the gift of sleep is by getting up early.

We are to seek first the kingdom and sleep is added to us, just like other kingdom blessings. We are not to love our sleep apart from the Giver. "Love not sleep, lest thou come to poverty; open thine eyes, and thou shalt be satis-fied with bread" (Prov. 20:13).

At the end of the day, we are invited to consider the results. Just look at the scoreboard.

> I went by the field of the slothful, and by the vine-yard of the man void of understanding; And, lo, it was all grown over with thorns, and nettles had cov-ered the face thereof, and the stone wall thereof was broken down. Then I saw, and considered it well: I looked upon it, and received instruction. Yet a little sleep, a little slumber, a little folding of the hands to sleep: So shall thy poverty come as one that travelleth; and thy want as an armed man. (Prov. 24:30–34)

The real world is a hard place and is happy to give a certain kind of individual a drubbing. He may think he is wise—he watches art films until three in the morning—but poverty awaits him armed with clubs. Artiste or no, the poverty still comes. The wise man received instruction by looking at the *field*. He did not have to catch the lazy man in the act of napping; he gathered wisdom from the results or lack of them.

The flip side of this is that hard work, real work, brings the blessing of sleep. "The sleep of a labouring man is sweet, whether he eat little or much: but the abundance of the rich will not suffer him to sleep" (Eccl. 5:12). Important lessons can be learned in work that makes you sweat, but the ethic transfers. Work, and eat your *own* bread (2 Thes. 3:12). Often, the rich work, but they work by shuffling their worries around on a desk, and then, not surprisingly, have trouble getting to sleep. The laboring man, whose life is far more simple, has worked hard and enjoys sweet sleep. Productive work for others (to be distinguished from high-stress, pointless work) is far more likely to be blessed at the end of the day with genuine rest and sleep.

ANXIETY

One of the things that robs Christians of sleep is worry. But take care as we consider this. It would not be fruitful to begin worrying about whether one worries too much.

> Stand in awe, and sin not: commune with your own heart upon your bed, and be still. Selah. Offer the sacrifices of righteousness, and put your trust in the LORD. . . . I will both lay me down in peace, and sleep: for thou, LORD, only makest me dwell in safety. (Ps. 4:4–5,8)

We have to learn some basic lessons here about trust and anxiety. The first lesson concerns a basic assumption about God. "Humble yourselves therefore under the mighty hand of God, that he may exalt you in due time: Casting all your care upon him; *for he careth for you*" (1 Pet. 5:6–7). Too many Christians have cultivated a view of God (which ironically, they think is a *high* view) in which they think God is stingy with His love, salvation, answers to prayer, and so on. But fundamental to right living before God is the recognition that God cares for us. He loves us. Some Christians have reacted to the common sentimentalism of pop evangelicalism by emphasizing that God is righteous, holy, and angry at sin. All this is scriptural in its place, but we must note that God is tender with His people, and He is tender to their children.

In the second lesson, we must learn the difference between a helmet and a head.

> Be careful for nothing; but in every thing by prayer
> and supplication with thanksgiving let your requests
> be made known unto God. And the peace of God,
> which passeth all understanding, shall keep your
> hearts and minds through Christ Jesus. (Phil. 4:6–7)

The peace of God protects us, not the other way around. Too many Christians try to deal with their anxieties by worrying on their knees. They worry, conclude it with "in Jesus' name, amen," and then, not surprisingly, have trouble sleeping. They have reversed the promise of this passage and tried to orient their hearts and minds in such a way as to "keep" or protect the peace of God. The peace of God is thought to be some kind of guttering candle, and the Christian must surround it with a serene heart and mind so that the peace of God won't blow out. But the promise is the other way around. The peace of God *which makes no sense* will guard our hearts and minds in Christ Jesus. The peace of God is the helmet, not the head. It's the thing which protects, not the thing protected.

The thing we must do as we seek this blessing is to be anxious for nothing, present our petitions to the Lord with thanksgiving. Many times we present our petitions, and then spend the next three hours tossing and turning. Far better to present those petitions, sing a psalm or a hymn with gratitude, and then go to sleep.

Think of it this way. If the devil is keeping you from sleep, or waking you up, behave in such a manner as to thoroughly discourage him. He will wake you up to get you to worry in your prayers—a sight that is probably a lot of fun to watch. But he won't get you up so you can sing psalms of gratitude. There is no return in it for him.

ENDS AND ODDS

Like every other aspect of our lives, our sanctification in sleep is part of our spiritual discipline. We work for it, we work with it, we work toward it. But godly work is always in the surrounding context of *grace*. We work out what God works in (Phil. 2:12–13). God saved us by His grace so that we could walk in good works, which He prepared beforehand for us to do (Eph. 2:8–10).

With this in mind, here are a few final points of application. Remember, grace is the context. Work so that your *body* is ready for sleep, and you can honestly ask for God's blessing. Work so that your *mind* is ready for sleep, and your anxieties have been cast upon Him. Work so that your *bedroom* and bed are ready for sleep—can you ask for God's blessing here? The state of your bedroom is a good metaphor for the state of your soul.

Given this, and the fact that you are teaching your children all these important lessons, learn to say grace before sleep. Learn also to bestow a blessing on your children when you put them to bed. The practice of praying before sleep is widespread and common. "Now I lay me down to sleep. . . ." I want to encourage parents, particularly fathers, to begin blessing their children. This means placing your hands upon their heads and praying for them, calling down God's blessings upon them. This includes the blessings of sound sleep, good dreams, waking refreshed, and spiritual and physical protection while they are vulnerable in their sleep.

THE SICKBED

There are a number of temptations that confront us when we are dealing with our health. Just a few comments are in order here. A complete treatment will have to wait for another time.

It should go without saying that parents should have some sort of functional medical knowledge. They are the ones who have to make countless decisions related to health: home treatments, whether to go to the doctor, whether to send the sick kid to school, and so on. As with so many other issues, cultivated wisdom in one area translates elsewhere.

Parents should be aware of *hypochondria*. Faking illness (even to oneself) is a tried and tested method for getting out of work, school, or responsibility. It's also used to get attention and sympathy that the invalid may believe is due him. Sometimes, for the sake of "honesty," a minor symptom is fanned into flame so that a child can accurately say that he has a sore throat. After all, he feels *something* down there.

But there is also the *opposite* of hypochondria; faking health rather than going to a doctor (or taking medication) is also a bad business. There are basic stewardship issues here as well as basic concerns of charity. For example, postponing an inevitable (but now far more serious) treatment is not a good way for fathers to provide for their families.

Disagreements between households over alternative and conventional medical treatments are also a problem. Sometimes such disagreements can also flare up within a household. Say that mom is sold on some alternative treatment, and the teenaged children are chafing under a regime of St. John's wort. The biblical principles that should be remembered here can be divided into two categories—

orthodoxy and charity. If a family is convinced of a particular medical treatment, they ought not to go on a crusade through their family and friends. This is the principle of charity. Of course friends and families should feel free to share what they have learned about something or other, but frequently sharing turns into hard-sell *sharing*. This is a sin against charity. It's also worth nothing that many medical treatments have been corrupted by false doctrines. In the alternative world, there is much New Age mysticism, and in the world of conventional medicine, there have been many compromises with a secularist scientism. This is a question of orthodoxy, and Christians have to be careful wherever they go.

At the foundation of everything, we find the principle of contentment. We live in a fallen world, and we are all going to die of *something*. We do not have a guaranteed "right" to health. Paul learned this lesson well (Phil. 4:11), as should we. Biblical homes often contain sickbeds, and even here, whether we are patient or nurse, we are to remember, "My life for yours."

CHAPTER THIRTEEN

The Deathbed

I believed, therefore have I spoken: I was greatly afflicted: I said in my haste, All men are liars. What shall I render unto the LORD *for all his benefits toward me? I will take the cup of salvation, and call upon the name of the* LORD. *I will pay my vows unto the* LORD *now in the presence of all his people. Precious in the sight of the* LORD *is the death of his saints. O* LORD, *truly I am thy servant; I am thy servant, and the son of thine handmaid: thou hast loosed my bonds. I will offer to thee the sacrifice of thanksgiving, and will call upon the name of the* LORD. *I will pay my vows unto the* LORD *now in the presence of all his people, In the courts of the* LORD's *house, in the midst of thee, O Jerusalem. Praise ye the* LORD. *(Ps. 116:10–19)*

As we consider home life, we must recognize that circumstances vary—whether from home to home, life to life, or culture to culture. But one of these variations supplied by our technocratic culture has created something of an optical illusion. We have a tendency to want to get death *away* from our homes and families and off to some "dying place." But we need to realize that one of God's great gifts to His people is the death bed at home. A death away from home can certainly be honorable, particularly death in battle, but to be full of years and be gathered to your people while among your people is a tremendous blessing.

In our passage, we speak the way we believe (116:10), and we speak on our deathbeds the way we *have* believed.

This is another way of saying we die as we have lived. Man is born to trouble as the sparks fly upward, but it's too easy to be cynical. It's hasty to say all men are false (Ps. 116:11). At the end of one's life, the mind should turn naturally to thanksgiving—what can we give the Lord for all His benefits (116:12)? A good way to end one's life is by taking up the cup of salvation, calling upon God, and paying vows in the congregation (116:13–14). God's perspective of death is different from ours (116:15). Complete submission to His will in this is appropriate (116:16), and presenting thanks to God is fitting (116:17). Praise in the congregation is a wonderful conclusion to life (116:18–19) because the departing saint is being gathered into a much *greater* congregation.

GATHERED TO HIS PEOPLE

The Bible gives us a wonderful image of this death of saints, a death which is precious in the sight of God. Because it is precious in the sight of God, and because we say *amen* to all His decrees, such deaths should be precious in our sight as well. We do this by faith, and not by sight. Consider:

> Then Abraham gave up the ghost, and died in a good old age, an old man, and full of years; and was gathered to his people. (Gen. 25:8)

> And Isaac gave up the ghost, and died, and was gathered unto his people, being old and full of days: and his sons Esau and Jacob buried him. (Gen. 35:29)

> And when Jacob had made an end of commanding his sons, he gathered up his feet into the bed, and yielded up the ghost, and was gathered unto his people. (Gen. 49:33)

We tend to think of death as the time we are separated from our people, but the Scriptures say it's the time we are *gathered* to our people. For those who see with the eyes of faith, death is a gathering time, not a sundering time.

A MOMENTARY GRIEF

At the same time, it is certainly appropriate and right for Christians to grieve at the loss of someone dear to us. We grieve, but our grief is to be *as free of unbelief* as the rest of our lives. Grief is part of what must be sanctified in us. This is the direct teaching of Paul. "But I would not have you to be ignorant, brethren, concerning them which are asleep, that ye sorrow not, even as others which have no hope" (1 Thes. 4:13). We may sorrow, but it must be sorrow in perspective. We grieve over the momentary separation, but it's the sort of sorrow you might observe at an airport when a family is bidding farewell to a loved one for a period of many years. They know they will be together again, but the temporary separation (as far as *this* life is concerned) is still very real (Acts 20:38). We must always keep the balances held upright (2 Cor. 4:17). Death has really been conquered (Heb. 2:14; 1 Cor. 15:55–57).

The basis of Christian grief is separation, not annihilation. We are not like pagans who are without God and without hope in the world. This means that all things will be restored, the dead will be raised, and the reunions will happen. Just as the grief seen when loved ones separate at airports is a small type of death, so the joy seen at reunions is a small type of the resurrection.

Those who are without God and without hope generally fall into two categories, and Christians must be careful to avoid both of them. One is a morbid fascination with death and an inability to stay off the subject. The other is a fearful repression of the entire subject and a refusal to think about it or deal with it in any responsible way.

PRACTICAL CONCERNS

We should therefore think in a distinctively biblical way as we approach the subject of death and dying.

Everything else being equal, it's better to die at home than not. It is good to be with your people as you are gathered to your people. Sometimes nursing homes or hospitals are a medical necessity, and so dying at home is a blessing to pray for, *not a rule to observe*. If someone spends his last days in a hospital, this is not because someone is "sinning." But being able to die at home is in fact a great blessing, and hospice care is a wonderful work for Christians to be involved in.

Families that sacrifice to make this happen are not robbing their children or anyone else; they are giving to everyone involved. A death at home is not something that should be assumed as traumatizing for the children. If the adults involved meet the situation with love, faith, and appropriate grief, the children will learn what they must learn.

We want to die the way we have sought to live—honestly. This means lying to the person with the terminal condition is out. If the person is ready to meet God, the truth is precious. If they are not ready to meet him, the truth is most necessary.

This last point reveals the lying heart of the euthanasia movement. In many of the so-called "death with dignity" debates, we are told the law should recognize someone's right to suicide because it will "end their suffering." Note that this means the state is being asked to assume that such a death will in fact end the suffering. But for Christians, if someone dies in unbelief and rebellion, that moment is the eschatological *beginning* of their sufferings.

Pain medications are lawful and a great mercy. But we must remember that the point of all such medications should be to keep the patient *as clearheaded as possible*. We should desire that our dying might be a strenuous reaching for the finish line (2 Tim. 4:7–8). Medications that interfere with clear thought should be avoided as much as possible, so long as we note that extreme pain also interferes with clear thought. Our goal should be to die well, and medications that help with this are to be sought. Medications that ensure someone finishes their days in a chemical fog unnecessarily should be avoided.

The Bible does not absolutely prohibit cremation (and so neither should we). Sometimes this might be thought to be a financial necessity, but at the same time, the Scriptures do indicate in various places that burial is a wonderful testimony to our faith in the resurrection of the dead (Heb. 11:22). Burial is a basic Christian testimony, and the government-regulated funeral home racket has done a great deal to damage this testimony. How many churches that are being built today have a churchyard connected to them?

CONCLUSION
The house of mourning is a good place to learn wisdom. It's good to be reminded of our own mortality. We don't want to be morbid, but each of us needs to know we will die (Eccl. 7:4). This is an inevitable event, and it's one which requires thoughtful preparation.

Look at your hands, holding this book. Those hands will one day be bones. What does this bring to mind? God is good and God is sovereign. To dust we all shall return, and glory to God. We surrender gladly to the principle He has established—my life for yours.

CHAPTER FOURTEEN

The Kids' Bedrooms

Children, obey your parents in the Lord: for this is right. (Eph. 6:1)

Children, obey your parents in all things: for this is well pleasing unto the Lord. (Col. 3:20)

As we have worked our way through a biblical household, the emphasis necessarily has been on parental responsibilities and duties. But this should not lead anyone to believe these are the only responsibilities within the home. One good place to highlight the responsibilities of children is their "space"—their bedrooms.

We all know the broader context of this, which is the responsibilities of parents, specifically fathers. But we have a tendency to link our obedience to the obedience of others, which these texts don't do. It does not say, "Children, obey your parents *if* they do this or that."

Note a few important details about these verses. First, they are addressed to *children*, that is, those who are under their parents' care and oversight. Such children are assumed to be a functioning part of the congregations at Ephesus and Colossae. Second, obedience is to be rendered to the *parents*, which means both of them. Father and mother individually and together are to receive the obedience of their children. This obligation relates to the neighboring requirement of honoring parents, which should not require force. If honor is rendered only with coercion, then something is seriously wrong. Third, it's *obedience* that is required. And last, it's the right thing to do and is *well-pleasing* to the Lord.

INSIDE AND OUTSIDE

One of the central things we should want young people to learn (so that they will not have to *unlearn* so much as we have had to do) is the integration of the inner and outer aspects of their lives. The hypocrite cleans up the outside because it's easier than cleaning up the inside (Mt. 23:25). But while this sin will always occur to the end of the world, it's currently far less common than its opposite gnostic error, which is the assumption that if the inside is "fine," then the outside is basically irrelevant.

Dependent children need to understand that their environment is their life—this includes thoughts, notebook, bedroom, and heart. What a child does with his body is just as much a part of his spiritual life as his prayers are (Rom. 12:1–2). This includes making the bed (or not), picking up socks (or not), or doing homework in the bedroom (or not). This must be emphasized because neglect of it is why so many good Christian kids feel that when they disobey they are not "really" disobeying. We've been trained in such a way as to think that if we honor our parents "on the inside," we're "really" honoring and obeying them, whether or not we actually are.

LISTEN UP

The word for *obey* used in both these verses is *hupakouo*. This is important because of the role *listening* has in the word. Now of course, kids are not required to be mind-readers. If a child is in the backyard, and his mother goes into his closet and whispers instructions about cleaning it up, the child is not in sin because he didn't hear her. But (let's be honest) this is not what usually happens.

One of the uses of this word in Scripture refers to a porter, whose *job* is to listen for a knock at the door. His first act of obedience is to *hear* the command. Just as "I forgot" is not a biblical excuse, neither is "I didn't hear you." An obedient child is one who is *eager to hear* the instructions.

PRACTICAL CONSIDERATIONS

So what should obedience look like? What are some key principles that children need to master?

First, *obedience is not hard of hearing*. As noted, an obedient heart listens for the command and *wants* to hear it. This, more than anything else, reveals whether an obedient disposition is present. A reluctant heart may be constrained to do whatever was required, but a reluctant heart almost never hears with alacrity. The same point about hearing quickly is made in another metaphor, a visual image found in the Psalms. "Behold, as the eyes of servants look unto the hand of their masters, and as the eyes of a maiden unto the hand of her mistress; so our eyes wait upon the LORD our God, until that he have mercy upon us" (Ps. 123:2). So deaf obedience is disobedience.

Second, *obedience is not forgetful*. If a child is told to make his bed on Monday, this command doesn't evaporate by Wednesday. Two days of disobedience do not nullify the command. Children have a natural and lamentable tendency to consider lack of action by the parents as a form of tacit permission. Forgetful obedience is disobedience.

Third, *obedience is not piecemeal*. The Colossians passage says that children must obey parents *in all things*. If given a list of things to do, accomplishing half of them is not obedience. If a father tells his son to mow the lawn and trim the hedge, and instead, the son trims the hedge and plays video games, the result is simple disobedience. Partial obedience is disobedience.

Fourth, *obedience is not postponed.* Attempts to set an independent schedule for obedience is simply another way of seeking to wrest control of the whole thing away from the parents. We learn this lesson from what God tells us through the author of Hebrews: today if you hear His voice, do not harden your hearts (Heb. 3:7–8). Delayed obedience is disobedience.

Fifth, *obedience is not subject to private interpretations.* It's easy to begin thinking things like, "I don't have to do this because I am older now." In other words, "older than I was two months ago." In the political realm this sort of thing is called *spin.* A child should not be allowed to spin the requirements placed upon him so that they are more to his liking. A child should not be allowed to do this sort of thing until after they have grown up and become a Supreme Court justice. Reinterpreted obedience is disobedience.

Sixth, *obedience is not reluctant or sullen.* If obedience is well-pleasing to God, then it's to be well-pleasing to us. This of course relates to the first consideration, which is that of eagerness to obey. But someone might obey right away (out of fear, say) and still not like it, so grumpy obedience is disobedience.

APPLICATION
Two concluding considerations. Christian children should know, and their parents should know, that they are being brought up to *maturity.* Once they have grown to mature adulthood, they will be in their own households, and they are then to honor their parents differently—and this will no longer be through obedience. But now, while they are still at home, they will go through a time of transition as they grow toward that independence. Take care that children grow toward maturity *in* all maturity, which means that young people should not request the privileges of maturity first. Wisdom dictates that they should request the responsibilities first. In other words, a teenager should *not*

say, "Dad, I am sixteen now, and I think I should be able to stay out with my friends until midnight." The issue is not whether it's bad to stay out until midnight but the fact that the young person is crawling backwards into maturity. Request responsibilities first, and all these other things will be added. "Dad, I am sixteen now. Do you think I might be able to take over my car insurance payments?"

Related to this, young people should strive to see their lives as an integrated whole. If the "heart is right," but the bedroom is a pit, then this is not happening. If the room is spotless, but the heart is filled with all manner of uncleanness, then it's not happening either. Our children must learn to avoid Pharisaical hypocrisy at the same time they are rejecting gnostic mysticism. This is shorthand for "clean your room with a clean heart."

The Guest Room

Let love be without hypocrisy. Abhor what is evil. Cling to what is good. Be kindly affectionate to one another with brotherly love, in honor giving preference to one another; not lagging in diligence, fervent in spirit, serving the Lord; rejoicing in hope, patient in tribulation, continuing steadfastly in prayer; distributing to the needs of the saints, given to hospitality. (Rom. 12:9–13)

Hospitality, where it is still practiced in the church, is largely an *unstudied* virtue. The demands of modernity and the frenetic pace of life around us dictate that we neglect our responsibility to have our brothers and sisters into our homes. Nevertheless, the Bible is very plain in requiring us to be disciplined in our pursuit of "company," and includes a requirement of hospitality in the leaders of the church (1 Tim. 3:2). This is not because it's their task alone but rather because a pattern or example should be set by them for the whole church.

Before addressing the duties related to hospitality, just a few words are necessary to that group which always finds time to lament the unfriendliness and lack of hospitality in *others*. This duty is one where we may trust the Lord to convict us of our own failings. With regard to the purported failings of others, take care not to draw *any* conclusions about their hospitality. First, most of the time we are in no position to make a right judgment. Second, those who show great interest in the failings of others in this regard are usually a central part of the problem.

I have located our discussion of this important aspect of biblical living in the home under the heading of the "guest room," even though much biblical hospitality doesn't necessarily involve overnight guests. But whether guests are staying overnight, coming to dinner, or just dropping by for coffee, the biblical principles remain the same.

LOVE WITHOUT HYPOCRISY

In Romans 12:13, the saints are told to *pursue* hospitality, to chase down potential guests in the parking lot. Far more is involved in this than a simple *willingness* to have company over—Paul is saying that we must make it happen. But this occurs in the midst of a veritable cluster of virtues. He begins (12:9) by saying our love must be unhypocritical and then proceeds to show all the different ways an unhypocritical love is manifested. Opening your home is an essential part of this, and being hospitable on a regular basis is a Christian grace. This means we do not need to be concerned about the ill-effects of hospitality considered in itself. It's *not* bad for the kids. While it is possible to overdo it, this is not the problem most of us confront.

FERVENT LOVE

The context of hospitality is to be love—fervent love. The word for *fervent* does not refer to a fever pitch of emotional enthusiasm but rather to constant and continual exertion as an athlete running a race. A Christian people are to be dedicated to this. They are to think about how to use their house as an instrument that will enable them to pursue hospitality in a strenuous way.

The Bible says that love covers a multitude of sins. This is good because hospitality frequently *uncovers* a multitude of them. "And above all things have fervent charity among yourselves: for charity shall cover the multitude of sins. Use hospitality one to another without grudging" (1 Pet. 4:8–9). Peter tells us to be hospitable without begrudging it, without grumbling because God loves a cheerful giver. If you share your home with a bad attitude, you have the worst of every situation—no treasure in heaven and a lousy evening to boot!

DO NOT FORGET

Like the other biblical writers on this subject, the author of Hebrews places hospitality in the same context as our other writers on this subject, which is the familial love which God has granted to us as His children. Let brotherly love continue, he says, and *do not forget* to show hospitality (Heb. 13:1–2). In saying this, he is not promising us angelic visitations but rather unexpected blessings. Those who entertained angels were those saints of God in the Old Testament who had set an example of hospitality.

The Bible teaches that hospitality is an important way to advance the work of the kingdom of God, so if we pray for God's kingdom to come, we must be willing to open our doors. "We therefore ought to receive such, that we might be fellow helpers to the truth" (3 Jn. 8). By the same token, we are not to share the blessing of our table with false teachers (2 Jn. 10–11) or those under discipline (1 Cor. 5:9–13).

But as we undertake this, we should remember the admonition given us by C.S. Lewis. He once commented on a woman who lived for others—and you could identify those others by their hunted expression. The design of hospitality is to serve the needs of the guests and not to meet any personal emotional needs the hostess might have. This is not something which occurs in nature spontaneously. The Holy Spirit gives the impulse and desire, but like all the virtues, cultivation and discipline are most required.

CHAPTER SIXTEEN

The Entertainment Center

Thou blind Pharisee, cleanse first that which is within the cup and platter, that the outside of them may be clean also. (Mt. 23:26)

Finally, brethren, whatsoever things are true, whatsoever things are honest, whatsoever things are just, whatsoever things are pure, whatsoever things are lovely, whatsoever things are of good report; if there be any virtue, and if there be any praise, think on these things. Those things, which ye have both learned, and received, and heard, and seen in me, do: and the God of peace shall be with you. (Phil. 4:8–9)

Many American homes have an entertainment center located in the living room or family room. Our task here consists of learning how Christian discipleship relates to the vast ocean of entertainment options that surround us on every hand. Should you allow it into the home through an eye dropper? A funnel? Not at all? And most important, what is the *real* reason for any standards you set?

As we look at the two texts cited above, we find two very important principles. The first is that we are to love what is noble and praiseworthy. Our minds and hearts are to turn naturally to that which is virtuous and of good report. Our lives should feel a strong gravitational pull to that which is pure.

But this is just half the story. The higher the standard, if it's handled wrongly, the worse the legalism. Jesus does not oppose the outside and inside of the cup as though they constituted some sort of logical contradiction. He says cleaning the inside naturally results in a cleansing of the outside. But cleaning the outside alone does nothing but generate dualistic hypocrisy.

WISDOM BEFORE PARTICULARS

Wisdom can be severe at the beginning. Legalism is severe all the way through. However, it's a violation of biblical wisdom to confuse the two in any way. Yet this is done all the time by those who are immature. Legalism masquerades as wisdom. The wise are accused of being legalists.

Wisdom can see things in the text that cannot be seen by the immature. Legalism can see things in the text that the mature cannot see. How are we to tell the difference? Apart from wisdom, there is no way to do this. "But strong meat belongeth to them that are of full age, even those who by reason of use have their senses exercised to discern both good and evil" (Heb. 5:14).

On all such questions, the center of wisdom is an understanding of this inside/out dynamic. The *way* we are to grow into our standards is far more important than the standards themselves. Wisdom is a soil in which godly standards grow. Standards apart from wisdom are trying to grow in no soil at all, suspended in midair.

Young Christians can readily see what older Christians are doing or not doing. They drink this kind of beer, not that kind. They watched this movie but not the other one. They listen to a particular kind of music and avoid another kind of music. Now with this data, the younger Christians can readily draw the wrong inferences because what they cannot see is what makes all the difference. Wisdom addresses *why* they do what they do and the *way* they do it. This is not nearly so apparent, and so rather than trying to find out about that wisdom, the one who would follow their example settles for copying what he can readily see, which is the outside.

GROWING UP INTO WISDOM

This dynamic of younger Christians imitating older Christians can be seen in a stark way when it comes to bringing up children. The wisdom shown by the parents is not necessarily wisdom *felt* by the children. As parents bring up their children, a certain level of "outside/inness" cannot be escaped for the time being. The parents say, "No, we don't watch that kind of movie." The child doesn't yet know why (inside), but he does know (outside) he isn't watching it.

This is perfectly all right if the parents understand the direction they are going. The imposed standards are training wheels and are meant to come off. As we have emphasized in other contexts, external standards in childrearing should *decrease* as time goes on—and not because they are going away. The decrease only seems that way to others because the standards are being internalized. Explicit standards may have to be imposed on an eleven-year-old, but if that imposition is still necessary seven years later, then it's because the parents have failed to teach wisdom.

Another way of putting this is to say the goal of parents in teaching entertainment standards to children should be to have the outside behavior of a sixteen-year-old child governed by the child's internalized standards. If the external behavior is governed by the external rules imposed by the parents (beyond the training wheels stage), then the parents should confess this as their failure first, not the child's.

These standards begin as rules, move on to rules accompanied by teaching, move on to teaching alone, and then move on to the joy of watching your children begin the process over again by establishing some training wheel rules for their little ones.

ALL THIS SAID, SOME PRINCIPLES

The perils of getting this whole thing backwards should not prevent us from eventually getting to the particulars.

The first and most important principle is that *Scripture is the embodied standard.* Our standard is not to be a goopy and sentimental Victorianism. Neither is the standard something cooked up by unbelievers in Hollywood. What could PG-13 possibly mean in scriptural terms? And this must take us well past a disapproving frown about something or other, justified with a decontextualized proof text. In other words, there is plenty in Scripture that could earn us a hard R rating, and there is plenty in pop entertainment that is soundly condemned by Scripture. We have to learn to think like Christians across the board. Too often we raise the cry *sola Scriptura* when it really ought to be *tota et sola Sciptura.* All of Scripture and only Scripture is to be our infallible and ultimate court of appeal. Is it a sin to have a character in a fictional piece violate the third commandment by taking the name of the Lord in vain? Then why did Jesus have one of His characters in a parable sin in that way (Lk. 18:11)? Isn't the crass humor found in so much comedy relatively harmless? Then why did Paul forbid having anything to do with it (Eph. 5:4)? Life is not as simple as the legalists would like it to be.

Another important principle to note is that *narrative shapes us.* As in Philippians 4:9, we are not to think about the pure, lovely, virtuous, etc., so that pleasant liquids might slosh around in the jars of our minds. Narrative results in doing. copycat crimes and stunts are therefore not an example of people being idiots; they are examples of people being people but shaped by the wrong kinds of narrative. This means those who say they have the ability to "turn off" the power of the narrative to shape them are both unnatural and deluded. The stories we watch and read do *not* float on the surface of our lives like leaves on a pond. Every narrative subverts competing narratives, and part of the way this is done is through shaping those who lend their ear to the narrative, thus committing themselves to become like the story.

A third principle is that *sex and violence are not twin evils*. First, they are not evils. They are good or evil, *depending*. The virtue or vice depends on the direct object. As Lenin once put it, "Who? Whom?" Secondly, they are not twins. The propriety of showing them varies. For example, public sex is degrading (1 Cor. 10:7–8), while private violence is degrading (Gen. 4:8). In our day, we have reversed this. Instead of public hangings in the public square, we execute prisoners in the middle of the night in the inner recesses of the state penitentiary, and back in the public square, we find ourselves looking at an enormous billboard of some woman who is almost wearing something.

Yet another principle is that *language is contextual*. A simplistic "outside-in" approach focuses on a list of "bad words" as though there were such a list of prohibited vocabulary up in heaven. At the same time, we ought not ignore the shaping power of language. If a man writes a story in which a character steals, this doesn't make the author a thief, and this is why Jesus was not guilty of breaking the third commandment because one of His characters did. Language is directional, not static. It takes us somewhere, and we ought to be asking more questions about the road we are on and fewer questions about the color of paint on the car.

And last, *virtue is not the absence of vice*. Virtue is the active *presence* of something. That "something" is always distasteful to those who are uninterested in wisdom or holiness. Superficial analysis always gravitates to what the show "didn't have." This kind of approach usually winds up taking out the big chunks of ungodliness and then drinking the broth.

.

CHAPTER SEVENTEEN

The Junk Drawer

*At Parbar westward, four at the causeway, and two at
Parbar. These are the divisions of the porters among
the sons of Kore, and among the sons of Merari.*
(1 Chr. 26:18–19)

STRICT OR LOOSE?
Christian parents often present themselves with a false alternative when it comes to how they love their children through discipline. That false alternative is the choice presented between "strict" and "loose." Strict parents are assumed to be the more conservative and biblical, while loose parents are believed to be compromised in their standards. The tragedy is that both are equally missing the mark— Jesus frequently had looser standards than the Pharisees but those "loose" standards of His did not mean moral laxity. They actually represented a higher standard.

The task confronting parents is not to get children to conform to the standard the parents believe to be biblical. The task is to bring the children *to love* that biblical standard. At the very center of childrearing, therefore, is the question of inculcating loyalty. A covenant family cannot stay together without loyalty. But loyalty is a function of deep gratitude, and gratitude is a function of grace. Many parents, therefore, need to learn what it means to lighten up to the glory of God.

GRACE FREELY

So loyalty is a function of deep gratitude, and gratitude is a function of grace. Parents are to inculcate this sense of gratitude and thanksgiving by extending grace to their children. In this, the manner and attitude of the gift is crucial. Grace must be extended graciously. It's important for parents to nurture an atmosphere in which they constantly give to their children, and in which they do so freely. But it's important to distinguish "giving freely" and "giving a lot." The widow that Jesus observed putting her small pennies into the offering was giving freely, but she was not giving a lot. Parents give freely in their attitude—and if they are churlish or resentful or overbearing, gratitude doesn't grow.

Parents are responsible to see that their children grow up as thankful human beings, but this is not necessarily the same thing as growing up as indebted human beings. Gratitude liberates, while debts of every kind weigh us down.

THE GARDEN OF EDEN

When God placed Adam in the garden, there was only one *no.* Adam and Eve could eat from any of the trees in the garden except for one. Our God is a God of grace, a God who gives to the point of overflow. This can be seen in how He created a garden where virtually every tree was a *yes.* Parents should remember this when their little ones become mobile and start life within their "garden." Given the nature of things, there do need to be certain things that are off-limits for the kids for various reasons: toddlers shouldn't be able to play with electric sockets, and they shouldn't be allowed to kick the vase off the coffee table. Sometimes there even have to be points of testing *for* the point of testing. After all, God did place one tree in the garden that was off-limits. Even so, the attitude of parents should be one of grace, wanting to bestow, desiring to give. Unless their authority is respected, they cannot give, but authority can be established without having a tempting *no* every foot and a half. All this is another way of encouraging parents to toddler-proof the house with grace in mind.

RUNNY NOSES

When it comes to the care and feeding of children, practical neglect of them communicates a lack of love in two important ways. The first may be obvious—others look at the children in their unkempt state and rightly wonder if anyone loves them. But the second aspect of this is a self-fulfilling prophecy cycling downwards. When little children are not cared for properly, they regularly show up dirty, smelly, disheveled, and with a runny nose. In this condition, when some form of discipline is necessary, it's easy for some parents to communicate more than love and justice in the discipline. Rather, they communicate dislike or distaste. The unloveliness of the child (which the parents created) makes it harder to love the child when they need love the most, which is at the moment of discipline. The Bible says that when a brother is to be corrected, then the one correcting should be spiritual (Gal. 6:1). This applies to parents—especially to parents. So in all this, it's important for parents not to set up stumbling blocks for themselves.

BALANCE

The hardest thing in the world to maintain is ethical balance. Nowhere is this more evident than in the area of loving and disciplining children. The two obvious extremes in childrearing are laxity on the one hand and strict woodenness on the other. The natural tendency of people in each group is to point to the excesses of those in the other as justification for continuing on their own destructive course. Parents of banshees point to the uptight and are glad they are not like that. Parents of automatons point to the disorder of their opposing counterparts and are grateful they don't have those problems. But the point of childrearing is not order or disorder but rather love. Order that serves love is a delight. Disorder for the sake of others is also a delight. Wisdom alone establishes the point of equipoise.

READ SOME MORE!

Children need to hear stories. The reason is that they must learn to interpret stories, and they must do this so that they will come to understand the story of their own lives. The gospel story is of course the center of this process. But we learn to understand this story the same way we come to understand the language of Scripture. We learn language, and because of this, we can hear the language of God in Scripture. We learn stories, and therefore we learn to hear the gospel as a story. When children are steeped in stories, they learn that they are characters in a story as well. This kind of wisdom is the result of hearing countless stories: Bible stories, fairy stories, family stories, stories about work, short stories, humorous stories, serious stories, and many more. When children come to see themselves as characters, they then come to that wisdom which asks the really profound questions. "Am I a Peter? A Eustace? An Edmund? Am I Samwise? Lucy?" In short, they learn to ask what kind of character they are in the story being written all around them.

DOUBLE STANDARDS

Double standards are the enemy of all true religion. Nowhere is this more evident than in the home. One really effective way to scramble the kids is to demand from them what you are not demanding from yourself at the moment of correction. Immediate double standards can readily turn children into cynics. It's one thing to warn your children away from sins you may have committed twenty-five years ago—they can see that such warnings may come from long and godly experience—but it's quite another thing to demand patience from them in a loud and impatient voice. If you correct a bad attitude *with* a bad attitude, the lesson the child learns is not that bad attitudes are wrong. He learns that bad attitudes are wrong unless you have the upper hand. So then the kid clings sinfully to his bad attitude, and commences work on getting the upper hand.

MORE ON DOUBLE STANDARDS

So double standards are an enemy of effective discipline in the home. No one wants to hear a parent yelling that the children need to learn to keep quiet. But another enemy of effective discipline is the reluctance that some parents have to discipline at all because they are so aware of their own shortcomings. Because they are afraid of hypocrisy, they don't intervene at those places where their children desperately need to be corrected and taught. Children (particularly teenagers) will then exploit this, using lack of parental perfection as a reason for disregarding what they were told to do. Compare it to food and cooking. Perhaps a mother doesn't feel that her cooking is what it ought to be. This doesn't keep the children from needing food, and children need discipline just like they need food. So parental hypocrisy is one danger. But preferring "no discipline" to "imperfect discipline" is another.

LEADERSHIP

We are not necessarily being unscriptural when our language varies from that of Scripture, but it at least means we might be. This potential problem arises in the home, particularly when mom is critical of how dad is doing his job in teaching and disciplining the children. The phrase "spiritual leadership" is not synonymous with "headship," although rightly understood the latter certainly entails the former. But when "spiritual leadership" is used as a stand-alone phrase, it quite often gets filled up with meaning by a discontented wife. "My husband is not a spiritual leader" can mean that a husband is failing in his husbandly duties, scripturally defined, but it can also mean, "My husband is not leading in the direction I want him to go." In plain English, I want him to lead me and the children *so long as he does it my way*. So in some cases, the phrase should actually be, "I am not a spiritual follower."

CHOICES

We bring up our children a particular way, and other people within our church community don't necessarily do the same as we do. Multiple choices confront every diligent parent, beginning with how the baby comes into the world. Home birth or hospital birth? Get them home and the question of schedule feeding and demand feeding arises. Then, when they can get down solids, what kind of solids? Whole grain nature food or stuff with cool chemicals in it? Home made or store bought? Then, how do we educate them? Home school or Christian day school?

Whatever choices we make, those choices will be reflected in how our children grow and are shaped—sins and virtues together. As others in the covenant community legitimately evaluate our children—which is *not* gossiping about them—as prospective employees, or suitors for a daughter's hand, etc., they are doing what the sacrament of baptism demands of us all. All our children are baptized children, and this means we all have a stake in one another's lives. Our fundamental loyalty is there and not with the various methods of childrearing we all must choose.

LOVE AND OBEDIENCE

Every biblical home contains within it both love and obedience. Love without obedience is spineless and ultimately not love at all. Obedience without love is the dust of death. But we have to go beyond this. It's important for us to note that while both are present, one contains the other. Specifically, love is the context for obedience and not the other way around. Grace cannot flourish in a home of law, but law flourishes of necessity in a home of love. Jesus said that if we loved Him, we would keep His commandments. He did not say that if we kept His commandments, then we would love Him.

This has everything to do with bringing up children. There are different ways to state this, but the demeanor, disposition, or aroma of the home must be grace, favor, kindness, and love. In that setting, and only in that setting, is it safe to issue a requirement.

TEACHING AND LEARNING
When the Scriptures teach us that parents should teach their children, the flip side of this is that children should learn from their parents. This is obvious to virtually everyone when it comes to teaching little ones how to tie their shoes or ride their bikes. But at a certain point, an independent spirit kicks in, one typified by "Me do it." Wise parents do two things with this: the first is that they see this as a first step toward the ultimate goal, which is functioning independence. But the second thing is just as important; this mere desire for independence is not the same thing as successful independence. Again, this is easy to see when a small child insists on falling off the bike by himself.

It is more difficult to see (but just as present) in children of high school and college age who believe they have the world all figured out. It's more difficult because their intelligence, education, size, street smarts, and so on are deceiving in appearance. The vast majority of young people need far more direction than they act like they need.

LOVE AND ATTENTION

All parents have experienced the ebb and flow of ordinary life. In bringing up children, nothing is static; nothing stays put. This means that everything might be harmonious and smooth one week and then, a week or two later, mom and dad turn around to find discipline in disarray and insecurities sprouting everywhere. In such situations, parents should confer together and resolve before God to "pour it on." The first thing to pour on is love and attention, addressing all the attention-getting tricks that insecure kids instinctively know. When it comes to receiving love and attention, children are American SUVs—real gas guzzlers. This requires dedicated investment from the parents, but it's well worth it. It's far better than the alternative—little crumple cars that run on fumes and disintegrate when bumped.

The second thing to pour on is clear, defined, and reasonable discipline. Discipline by itself will not fix insecurity, but insecurity frequently comes from a lack of consistent, loving discipline.

LISTEN TO THE KIDS

An important part of bringing up children is the art of listening to them. Of course, when they volunteer things, it's important to hear, but I mean much more than this. Proverbs tells us that "counsel in the heart of man is like deep water; but a man of understanding will draw it out" (Prov. 20:5). There is a crucial application of this principle to our children if we would be parents "of understanding." Doing this is more a matter of the will than a matter of discovering some hidden technique. How do you draw your children out? *Ask questions.*

And parents need to learn how to ask questions of their children without having an immediate agenda. In other words, if parents start to ask questions, and the children immediately become wary, this is likely because asking questions is usually a prelude to a lecture or a rebuke. This is a generalization, but parents need to learn how to draw out "counsel" from their children without feeling obligated to do something about it on the spot. The point is that children should know how to enter a conversation with a father or mother, which is quite a different thing than entering a trap.

CHILDREN AND CONVERSION

How are we to understand the "conversion" of our children to God. We know they are, like us, descendents of Adam and therefore by nature under the wrath of God. Yet under the grace of God, they were born into covenant homes and are being raised in the nurture and admonition of the Lord. By nature they are from Adam, by grace they are from the second Adam.

Parents need to guard against two errors here, the first of which is very common in evangelical homes. That error places the burden of proof on the child who has to show that he is "really in." The other error presumptively maintains that any baptized child is "really in," regardless of flaming evidence to the contrary. As children grow up in Christian homes, they are to be taught faith, not presumption. They are to be taught faith, not doubts. And the only way this balance can be maintained is through . . . faith.

BELIEVING GOD

The duty of Christian parents is to bring their children up in the nurture and admonition of the Lord. This means, at the fundamental level, a central duty of parents is to teach their children to believe God. Unfortunately, many parents in the name of "higher spiritual standards" wind up teaching their children to doubt instead.

Let's say a small child comes up to his father or mother and says something along the lines of "I love Jesus." If the response is anything like, "Child, do you know what you are saying?" or "No, you don't," or "You're too young to know what you are saying," the child goes away having learned to doubt. "I thought I loved Jesus, but apparently I don't. I must learn to be more suspicious of myself." It doesn't take too much of this before a child might be chased away from faith altogether.

CHILDREN AT THE TABLE

As parents teach their children with each administration of the Lord's Supper, one of the central things they must teach is how to discern the Lord's body. This does not mean that the children (or anyone else) should try to "see" the Lord's body up on the table in front of the church. That is not the "body" being referred to. Paul is rebuking the Corinthians for failing to see the body of Christ *in one another*. This is why he points to the one loaf being a symbol of the congregation. We have one church, and that's why we have one loaf.

This means that children should be required to learn how to see the body of Christ in their fellow Christians. A good place to start is with their brothers and sisters. As they repent of a squabble in the car on the way to church, they are discerning the body. As they look up and down their family row and out across the church, they are learning to discern the body. They are in fellowship with these people and must not be upset with any of them. This is something that a small child can understand and do.

LOYALTY

As with everything, there is a right way and a wrong way to understand loyalty. This means it's very important to teach the principles of loyalty to your children rightly. Of course, all creaturely loyalties are structured hierarchically with our loyalty to God as the only absolute. But when we consider earthly loyalties—to family, church, community, and so forth—things always get messy. This is because the side to which we belong is not perfect, and the opposing side is not demonic. Now what? Biblical loyalty means cheerful submission, within defined limits, to imperfection.

If your children grow up as individualists, they will want the right to vote on things perpetually. This means they have standing loyalty only to their own opinion. This also necessitates submitting to imperfection. But when the imperfect thing is the individualist's own opinion, those imperfections are much harder for him to see.

This state of affairs often comes about as the result of reading the wrong books, hearing the wrong stories, learning the wrong lessons. Robert E. Lee opposed secession but also knew when his opinion became irrelevant. Trumpkin advised against utilizing Susan's magic horn but then volunteered to undertake a mission he disagreed with. This was because he knew the difference between giving advice and taking orders. "You've had my advice," he said, "and now is the time for orders." To fail to learn this important distinction will leave your children like the dwarves in The Last Battle, now shooting Calormen, now shooting horses. The dwarves are for the dwarves.

DETECTIVE WORK

One commonplace observation about parenting is how many professions are gathered up into that role. Cooking, cleaning, teaching, and so on, are all part of it. My point here is that parenting also includes detective work, courtroom procedures, and sentencing guidelines. Not only is this important for the sake of applying justice to the children, it is of central importance in teaching them what justice is like. Many adults have no idea what constitutes a just or unjust charge: what biblical principles should be remembered when someone is charged, and so forth. One of the reasons adults have such problems with this kind of thing is that they did not learn these principles as kids. They don't know how to process conflict as an adult, and so their children also grow up without understanding justice either. So the basics of biblical jurisprudence should all be practiced in the home. Two or three witnesses give us the requirement of independent confirmation (2 Cor. 13:1). If a child tattles to get a brother or sister in trouble, and the report turns out to be false, you shall do to him as he thought to do to his sibling (Deut. 19:19). Parents must take trouble to sort out conflicting stories (Deut. 19:18), however great the temptation to spank them all and let God sort it out (Prov. 18:13). A full opportunity must always be given for the defense even if the defense promises to be pretty thin (Prov. 18:17). And discipline, when meted out, should be sharp, painful and *over* (Heb. 12:11).

PRAYING DETECTIVES

Parents should use prayer as an investigative tool. Suppose the parents suspect that one of the children has lied about something to them, but they cannot prove it. It's important that parents not discipline blindly because the Bible teaches that every fact has to be established in the mouth of two or three witnesses. But God knows the truth about the matter, and the parents should pray asking God to provide them with all they need to know in order to be godly parents. If there is a hidden lie that needs to brought into the light and dealt with, the parents should ask God to do it. Of course, such a prayer offered in all honesty is a prayer that's offered up in the will of God. How would our loving Father *not* answer such a prayer? Too often the reason we don't ask is that we don't really want to know. We belong to that shortsighted school of car maintenance and repair— don't lift the hood if you don't want to know.

A CLEANSING

Parents who discipline their children faithfully and regularly need to know it's almost certain they still miss things. In other words, in a disciplined household, kids still get away with various forms of disobedience. But two other things follow as a result. Because the kids are disciplined regularly, they know the standard. Because of this they know they got away with something sinful and are consequently bothered with guilt. As this sense of guilt accumulates (either because of elapsed time or additional undetected sins), the result is sometimes that a child begins misbehaving as a means of provoking discipline. Whether the child can articulate it or not, he knows that discipline administered in love has a cleansing effect. Sometimes a "minor" infraction is meant by the child to help deal somehow with the sin he knows has been covered up. This means wise parents will have an eye out for this possibility. They will also take care not to hurry through a time of discipline in a perfunctory way. Good talks can result from studying your children.

PARENTAL SIN

Parents are sinners as well as children, and under the hand of the Lord, parents are children as well as children. This means everyone in the household, not just the kids, is under discipline. The kids must see this reality and not just acknowledge it in an abstract, doctrinal sense. Parents often fail at this point because they refuse to make restitution to their children. Let's say there's been a family quarrel and everyone loses their respective cool. Mom gets angry and yells, and the child is angry and defiant. Now what? Obviously, the object of the discipline is to get the child to seek forgiveness for sinning in this way, and there is someone there (mom or dad) to make sure it happens. But who will make mom confess her sin and seek forgiveness from the child? The answer is that the Holy Spirit does this. If parents never apologize, they are resisting the Holy Spirit. Sometimes parents don't seek forgiveness because they believe to do so would diminish their "moral authority." The truth is the only thing that diminishes moral authority is sin, and sinning without seeking forgiveness afterwards really puts moral authority into the tank.

SQUABBLES

Brothers and sisters quarrel and squabble with one another. Parents intervene, try to sort things out, and generally restore order. What happens when order is not really restored but moves into a low grade resentment? Parents need to watch for more than outbreaks of hostilities. Many sins run a low fever and don't attract the attention of a 104 degree fight. Such sins include things like envy, competition, taking offense, resentment, etc. On the opposing side of this, parental sins include favoritism or neglect. The low fever sins are those which necessitate that the children, when grown, will drift apart. This is the cause of many an adult "brother thing" or "sister thing." This is one more area where parents must watch, pray, exhort, and teach.

ODIOUS COMPARISONS

One of the more grievous sins committed by parents against their children is the sin of comparing them to one another. "Why can't you be more like your sister?" "Your older brother would never have done that." Children who are being disciplined do need to be compared but not to one of their siblings. The standard is always to be Scripture. If, for example, a child is disciplined for lying, and they are corrected because Scripture applies this standard to all of us, there is no partiality. But if a child is told his sister never told lies, then the parent is creating a number of awful temptations. First, the parent is sowing discord among the brethren, a sin God hates. Second, the parent is creating a temptation for the disciplined child to dismiss their parental judgment as biased and partial, a dismissal that has some factual basis. And third, when the parent is setting aside God's way of dispensing justice like this, it's not surprising when other, grosser forms of injustice are manifested in the family.

A LITURGY OF SPANKING

The liturgy of spanking often teaches as much as the spanking itself does. A child when grown will no doubt have forgotten all the various offenses he "caught it" for. But he will remember, and fairly clearly, how the process usually went. Even if he doesn't remember that process consciously, all he needs to do is wait until he begins disciplining his own children, and it will all come flooding back. Here is a suggested liturgy: First, the child has the offense explained to him. It's very important that this be calm and judicial and not done in anger. Then, the spanking is administered, with the swats varying according to the offense. Next, the child is held until he stops crying, the child is assured that everything is completely forgiven, and the world is a new place. Finally, parent and child pray together, thanking God for the forgiveness.

MEMORIES AND KNOWLEDGE

Most of what shapes the character of children as they grow will not be consciously remembered. Because we have been well-trained by certain rationalistic methods of education, we think someone doesn't "know" something unless he can reproduce it on a test. That kind of reproduction is certainly a minor form of knowledge and should not be disparaged. But in the Bible, a far more important aspect of knowledge is much closer to the bone than this. Children learn to speak a language fluently many years before the grammar of the thing is explained to them. A six-year-old child, fluent in English, could easily demonstrate fluency, while that same child would flunk a test *about* the language. This is an illustration of how children learn wisdom. Let him who is wise understand.

DEMEANOR

Language cannot be limited to the set boundaries of the propositional. The connotative value of words carries as much freight as the strict denotative value of words. In addition to this, many other aspects of our lives are constantly "speaking" also. They could be translated into propositions but when this happens, something is always lost in the translation. Parents are responsible to see to it their children learn to "speak" responsibly throughout every aspect of their lives. This ever-present language can be described by the word "demeanor."

For example, take a current fad for teenaged boys, the practice of not washing or combing one's hair for extended periods of time. This "bed-head" look is quite eloquent and speaks volumes of rebelliousness, individualism, old-fashioned dirt, and other forms of lost blogger poet unhappiness. Defending himself against objections from parents, the son might say, "But I am not saying any of those things!" By this he means that he is not saying any of them in audible sentences, but he is saying them nonetheless.

The reason many parents cannot get this through to their children is that the parents and children share a flawed approach to knowledge, and the children learned which from their now unhappy parents.

INESCAPABLE DISCIPLINE

The fact that discipline is occurring in a home doesn't mean the children are being disciplined in *godliness*. Often the standard of discipline is merely selfishness on the part of the parents. If you discipline children for selfish reasons, then that's what they learn. Everything rides on how it's done. Discipline applied from love teaches the child to avoid the prohibited behavior. Discipline applied from selfishness teaches the child to manipulate others in the same way as soon as he is able (which is usually sooner than later). Parents who are selfish as they discipline can frequently be identified by comments such as, "How could you do that to us?" and "Why are you being so rude?" (by implication, "to me"). The child learns that to be a grown-up is to have the right to be self-absorbed.

IMPOSSIBLE PARENTING
The task of parenting is simply impossible. Any sane look at what is required of parents by God is completely and utterly overwhelming. This is why the task must be undertaken in grace, by grace, through grace, and because of grace. The grace of God in this provides two things all parents need. The first is forgiveness for this morning, and the second is strength for this afternoon. The promises of God to parents were not given to sinless (and childless) angels. These promises were given to *us*.

There are many "diligent" parents who are not doing what they do by grace through faith. Here are some of the telltale indicators that grace-parenting is not happening: complacency, pride, guilt, and despair. Whenever we are confronted with any sin, we must confess and forsake it, and when we confess guilt-motivation in parenting, we must be careful to not wallow in guilt over it!

TEACHING MATH
Too many parents teach their kids to countdown to obedience. A child is told to do something, and he declines to obey. The parent repeats the command. The child just stands there. Then the parent says something like, "I'm going to count to three. . . ." This is not teaching obedience, it's

teaching math. And then if the parent is really a pushover, he moves into teaching fractions. "Two and a half. . . ." But what has changed between the command and the three? Nothing. The child knows exactly when the point of enforcement will come. Sometimes it is when the parent actually gets to three. Sometimes it is when a certain tone or decibel level gets into mom's voice. Sometimes it is when the parent uses the child's full name—middle name and all. But the thing that teaches is the discipline in association with the word. The word by itself is hollow.

PROVOKING TO WRATH

Scriptures tell fathers not to provoke their children to wrath (Eph. 6:4). As we consider this, we should note that there are other ways to do this besides poking them with a stick. One of the more common is to do the *opposite* of what God does for us. No temptation comes to us but what is common to man, and God sees to it that there is a way of escape. But many times parents run a child's day in such a way as to remove all resources from the child and then crack down on the child when their folly finally manifests itself. For example, it's simply foolish to keep a young child up three hours past bedtime in order to visit with friends and then discipline the child for crabbiness. Small children need to be loved and tended, and discipline must occur in this context. This means that parents should have a mental checklist, *particularly* before a child can talk effectively. Is the child tired? Hungry? Thirsty? This is not to excuse sin. Rather, it means that parents need to take care not to stumble a weaker brother.

A CURIOUS LAW

The Old Testament has a curious law (to the modern mind). When someone was flogged, an upper limit was placed on how far the discipline could go. "Forty stripes he may give him, and not exceed: lest, if he should exceed, and beat him above these with many stripes, then thy brother should seem vile unto thee" (Deut. 25:3). In other words, the dignity of the one being disciplined was to be kept in mind (and protected) from the beginning of the process to the end of it.

This principle is neglected by many parents who humiliate their children in addition to the discipline they actually administer. Discipline should be painful but not degrading. Some examples of things that could be more humiliating than they are painful (and therefore more disobedient than they are corrective) would include striking a child in the face, spanking in front of the rest of the family, upbraiding the child in front of others, and so on. Children of course need to be disciplined, but they should never be insulted. They may feel insulted or put upon, but that feeling should always be part of the bad attitude being addressed by the discipline. The feeling, in other words, should not be justified; the parents should not be objectively insulting or degrading the one who is being disciplined.

There are different ways to insult children. One is to substitute insult for discipline. "Your sister never acts like that." Yet another way for parents to stumble at this point is to apply discipline inappropriate to the age of the child. Discipline should be calm, judicious, and done in such a way that the form of discipline doesn't cause the one disciplined to "seem vile."

AN OPTICAL ILLUSION

Adolescent children present parents with an imposing optical illusion. Because children at this time look more like adults than toddlers and because they are eager for increased responsibility and independence, parents often assume that their need for reassurance, affection, and love is somehow tapering off. But actually, this is a time in their lives when they need a marked *increase* of such affection. It's easy for a father to hug a six-year-old boy and very difficult (for some fathers) to hug a fifteen-year-old boy. Words of praise that used to flow easily are now mysteriously stuck in the throat. And with girls there is an additional complicating factor. This is the time when little girls are developing into women and many men pull away from their daughters for fear of being misunderstood. But sons and daughters both should grow to maturity in an environment of love, respect, praise, affection, and more.

REAL EDUCATION

The process of education is one that concerns every faithful parent, and the goal of such education is to impart knowledge to the child—as long as that word "knowledge" is biblically defined. What should a well-educated Christian child know as the result of growing up in his home?

When we ask this question, our natural instinct is to turn to the kind of knowledge measured by SAT tests, but the bedrock knowledge parents are responsible to impart is an unreflective knowledge of the love of God. In short, covenant children should know "in the liver" that God loves them and will keep all His promises to them. They will come to know this through the instrument of parental love, and parental teaching that links the love they enjoy in the family with the love they enjoy in the family of God.

CHILDREN WHO FLOURISH

When we garden, we know what to look for in order to determine whether the plants are flourishing. If they are brown and lying lengthwise on the ground, we know they aren't doing well. If they're green and luxuriant, we know they're receiving what they need.

What things can parents look for to determine if their children are flourishing? Any list can only indicate the sorts of things we want to see; a list like this cannot be exhaustive. But children should like spending time with their parents. Children should be, taking one thing with another, cheerful. Children should have a strong sense of identification with the family, a strong sense of family loyalty. Children should be bursting with news.

ALL YOU NEED IS LOVE

The fundamental goal of childrearing concerns who and what they love. Some may want to substitute other verbs, thinking the children have been brought up well based on what they earn, what they think, and what they say. Of course, what we love will affect all these others, but who and what we love is still central.

The greatest commandment in Scripture comes in the context of a passage on childrearing. We are to love the Lord our God with all our hearts, souls, minds, and strength. We are to do this self-consciously, because in this passage we are responsible to teach our children how to do the same things. Love is a communicable attribute of parents.

SILENCE

It's quite true some children are more verbal than others. This means some children will naturally be quiet and yet be quite content. But there are many times when a child is not communicative with parents, not because of a natural disposition but because something is wrong. This quiet might be because they are afraid of the conversation turning into something else, like a quarrel, or they are afraid of their parents knowing about what is distressing them. This might be the result of shame, fear, or despair.

Not all children talk all the time, but all children are thinking about something all the time. If this is the case—and there are truly deep waters in a child's soul—parents have to be careful not to demand the child open up. It doesn't work that way.

SMART TODDLERS

One of the besetting sins of parents is to assume that little children (toddlers) know far less than they actually know. Little children are emotionally, spiritually, and intellectually sensitive. Inability to articulate what you know is not the same thing as not knowing it. Many parents have little children who cannot form a question and don't know how to say "trash can, pick up, floor," or "napkin." But at the same time, if the parents said, "Billy, will you pick up that napkin from the floor and put it in the trash can?" They trot off immediately and do it. The knowledge here is doing, not saying. In a similar way, children register if their parents are quarreling, worshipping, feasting, or laughing. The fact that they may not be able to express how they are sharing in the event doesn't mean they are not *full* partakers.

COMPETENT HUMILITY

Two things are difficult to mix together: competence and humility. This creates a quandary for parents when they consider the education of their children. Competence without humility creates an insufferable arrogance. Humility without competence creates an oozing and unctuous insecurity. Moreover, when parents are successful in teaching their children in this way, the result will often be misunderstanding from the surrounding world. What does confident humility look like exactly? These things should be monitored and measured by parents in the following manner as the children grow: First, do the children have humble confidence before God, primarily in public worship? Second, do the children have humble confidence in the home in relation to their parents and siblings? Third, do they have this humble confidence before their teachers and others who have daily contact with them? If the answer is *yes*, the rest of the watching world will sort itself out.

DIFFICULT OR GOOD?

As we educate our children and as we struggle to recover academic standards, we must take care not to equate "classical" with "strict." Still less should we equate "classical" with "irrationally strict." I say this because my involvement in the classical Christian school movement has brought me into contact with more than one classical Christian school from Hell. Learning Latin can be difficult. Eating driveway gravel is always difficult. Some foolish educators think this puts learning Latin and eating gravel into the same genus. Classical education involves far more than pounding the students into an erudite paste. Genuine classical education has high standards, but the highest standards are for the schools, not the students. One of those standards is that children should be taught in such a way that they come to love their teachers and what they are learning.

LOYALTY AGAIN

One mark of a healthy home is the fact that the members of it have an intense loyalty to the other members of it. Other factors are necessary, obviously, but in a godly home, this should certainly be present. This includes loyalty to the persons, reputations, and opinions of everyone else in the home. Included in the many practical aspects to this, are obedience, verbal respect, and defense, when appropriate.

CHAPTER EIGHTEEN

The Closet

She is not afraid of the snow for her household: for all her household are clothed with scarlet. She maketh herself coverings of tapestry; her clothing is silk and purple. (Prov. 31:21–22)

If he take him another wife; her food, her raiment, and her duty of marriage, shall he not diminish. (Exod. 21:10)

Our modern closets are full of casual clothes. We work very hard at being casual. It's a studied occupation of ours. But of course if we study anything, we should study it in the light of Scripture, and this is something we have not yet seriously done.

As we look at these texts together, we find that clothing is important in marriage. One of the ways Scripture restricted the aspiring and amorous polygamist was by denying him the right to take away anything essential from a first wife in order to give to a second. When we look at what could not be taken or diminished, we see three basic categories—food, clothing, and conjugal rights. The clear implication is that these three things are right at the center of a husband's duties toward his wife. If these things were necessary when the sub-biblical pattern of polygamy was tolerated, how much more is it necessary for monogamous Christian husbands? We also see in the passage in Proverbs that a good wife is responsible for managing this provision and clothing herself and her family.

NECESSARY ADJUSTMENTS

Since the industrial revolution made fabrics cheap and plentiful, women stopped weaving cloth as a household necessity. Many continued to work this way for aesthetic or recreational reasons, but the days of necessary "homespun" were past. This simply shifted the basic responsibility in clothing a family from manufacturing to shopping or to a combination of shopping and manufacturing (i.e. sewing).

However a family is clothed, a father and husband has a scriptural responsibility to provide his wife with the wherewithal to do her duty in this area. I am sorry to have to press the point, but men need to understand this means money for shopping. The money ought not to be given grudgingly or as a last resort whenever a clothing crisis erupts. A man needs to be *provident*; in other words, he should anticipate things like winter (an event which should not be a surprise by now), and the household budget should contain room for the necessary provisions.

The flip side of this, for the wives, is taking their responsibility in shopping seriously. Buying a bunch of unnecessary items is *not* saving the household money even if *all* of them were twenty percent off. But if a wife takes her calling and vocation seriously, she will do her husband good in this area, and she will do so all the days of his life (Prov. 31:12–13). Wives who shop responsibly are a tremendous asset to their homes. If I spend too much time in a department store (as in, more than five minutes), I start to feel like something hot and wet is crawling up my back. The fact that my wife is gifted in (*voluntarily*) going from one of these places to another in order to save our household unnecessary expense is priceless.

BASIC PRINCIPLES

As wives and mothers shop for their households, they should be asking and answering one of the basic questions to all Christian living as they make decisions about their purchases. That question is *by what standard?*

The answer for Christians is obviously the standard of Scripture, and believe it or not, we have a number of scriptural lessons about clothing. We often assume that the Bible says nothing about this subject because we really don't want to be told anything that might contradict our practice. But we must remember, as we search the Scriptures, the existence of a scriptural standard for clothing doesn't mean we all have to dress alike. We have to remember we are Trinitarians.

Our point is not that all clothing must be the same; rather, our point is that there is no neutrality. Ultimately, all people dress in such a way as to express their faith, whether they are Muslim, Buddhist, polytheistic, or Christian. A Trinitarian approach to this will of course be grounded in Scripture. This means that Christians will dress differently from one another, and one Christian will dress differently from time to time depending on the situation. We are after the principle. The development of a Christian uniform would be a denial of what we are trying to accomplish.

So, what are the principles? First, *clothing should be functional.* We see Jesus taking off His outer garment to wash the disciples' feet (Jn. 13:4,12). We see Peter doing something similar when fishing (Jn. 21:7). There is no biblical sense in putting on a suit to clean out the garage. Mothers who insist the kids change out of their church clothes before going out into the backyard to play are observing this principle.

Second, we see in the Bible that *clothing should be appropriate to the occasion.* We see clothing for festive occasions (Mt. 22:11–12), and we see clothing for mourning (Gen. 37:34). Clothing is a form of communication, and one of the things it communicates is respect (or disrespect). To show up at your grandfather's funeral in jeans and a torn T-shirt is an effective way to communicate disrespect, whether it was intended or not.

A third principle is that *clothing reflects social status*. In the Bible, we see peculiar clothes for captives (Deut. 21:13), for widows (Gen. 38:14), and so forth. We do the same thing today (although we like to pretend that we don't) with UPS drivers, burger joint workers, nurses and doctors, students, soldiers and sailors, and so on. This is why it's a good idea for students to have "school clothing" or uniforms—not because we want everyone in the world to wear the same uniform but rather because we want to honor the particular vocation Christian students have. We understand this well enough in other areas, and the reason it's controversial in many school settings is because people have a real resistance to honoring the education their children are receiving. But we all acknowledge the fact that special clothing *is* a form of honor. What would happen if a judge was told he couldn't wear a robe, that a robe was irrelevant actually, and that he was still a judge "in his heart"? Bringing it back to school, what would happen if all the boys on the basketball team were told they would not be given uniforms? When answering the inevitable storm of protest, what would they think if we simply repeated back to them all the arguments they used to protest a school uniform? Special clothing is an inescapable concept. It is not *whether* we will honor particular callings with special clothing, but rather *which* callings will be so honored—and which dishonored.

And last, *clothing should concern itself with the comfort of others*—this is simply a reiteration of the theme of the entire book—"my life for yours." We all dress for comfort but *whose*? Scripture teaches us to love our neighbors as ourselves. When we get up in the morning, we make decision to dress in a certain way. The casual imperative has taught us that we should make these decisions with our own comfort as the prime consideration. A more biblical approach would ask about the comfort of others. I don't take a piece of cloth, tie it around my neck, and cinch it up tight because I think it feels good. It should be done for *others.* That's why, if I am going down to the office to work when no one else is there, I feel free to suit myself—and it doesn't involve a necktie. However, if I am going to teach a class, my concern should be to honor the students there by wearing a tie. The goal should not be to honor myself but rather to honor them.

CLOTHING SINS
Not only do we need to remember the positive principles as we dress ourselves, we also need to avoid the temptations the Bible marks. This also means that as the father provides for the clothing, and as the mother selects the clothing, there will be ample opportunities for both parents to teach their children the scriptural *basis* for the selections. Done right, this means as the children grow older and begin shopping for themselves, they will understand what they are to pursue and what they are to avoid.

One of the first sins to avoid in clothing is the sin of arrogance. We are prohibited from arrogantly dismissing others on the basis of clothing (Jas. 2:2–3). So we should guard against arrogance in how we dress (Mt. 23:5). Returning to "standards" in dress doesn't remove sin from the human heart. Every culture has an approved standard of dress, and every sinner wants to take pride in having attained or surpassed that standard. A teenager can be inappropriately proud of her prom dress or inappropriately proud of her blue jeans with the torn knee. The problem is the pride, not what one is proud *of.* Many young people today will discipline a breach of the protocols of cool as severely as any *faux pas* was censured in the court of Louis XIV.

Scripture also warns against *ostentatious immodesty.* Women are particularly warned against dressing themselves in a flamboyant manner (1 Tim. 2:9; 1 Pet. 3:3–4). At the same time, we need to remember our text (Prov. 31:22). This means that avoiding the sin of flamboyance doesn't require a pious dowdiness. But it does mean trying not to look like a circus horse.

Another kind of immodesty to be avoided is *sexual immodesty*. The Scriptures require Christian men to avoid lustful thoughts toward women generally (Mt. 5:28). Ungodly women have figured out many ways to help men disobey this command, and a lot of the tricks of the trade can be purchased at a department store near you. Actually, it is often the case that very little else can be purchased. Christian women frequently have to track down a merchant ship from afar in order to find anything decent for their teenage girls to wear. Christian women and girls who mimic the same tricks will get the same results. A number of Christian women need to stop playing dumb.

Modesty in this sense does not require that Christians dress in an androgynous fashion, obscuring the differences between men and women. Mothers should teach their daughters to dress in a way that's attractive without *attracting*. This means that clothes which incite, taunt, provoke, or invite are out. While shopping for clothes, girls should be taught that they have a sinful tendency to want to be lusted after, and they must learn to discipline themselves to resist this temptation. They must also learn that resisting this temptation involves understanding the reason for bare midriffs, the reason for tight shirts, the reason their slacks are cut the way they are, and so on. If mothers and daughters don't take a close look at the back of those jeans, they can rest assured plenty of others will.

Another sin to be avoided in dress is the sin of *worldliness*. The Bible never tells us to make sure our clothing is "cool." But neither does it prohibit understanding and conforming to the current fashion, unless the current fashion or style is driven by something which the Scriptures call worldliness (1 Jn. 2:15–17). Worldliness is an attitude and can only be dealt with at that level. Two people can wear the same clothes, the first is worldly and the other is not. This cannot be dealt with by a rule but rather by the Spirit and by wisdom. If the kids are *desperate* to have a particular "look" or logo, the hook of worldliness is in deep. The issue is not the logo but rather the desperation. And that's where wise parents should direct their attention.

SPIRITUAL CONDITION

Like it or not, our spiritual condition is reflected in the clothing we wear. We should think about this more than we currently do. When the patriarch Jacob was doing a little spiritual housecleaning, note what he told everyone to do. "Then Jacob said unto his household, and to all that were with him, Put away the strange gods that are among you, and be clean, *and change your garments*" (Gen. 35:2).

Strange garments are often the vanguard of strange gods. Repentance sees the connection as well. We see how much relativism has spread throughout the entire church. "Strange garments? Strange garments? Who is to say what is *strange*?"

CHAPTER NINETEEN

The Bathroom

Thou shalt have a place also without the camp, whither
thou shalt go forth abroad: And thou shalt have a paddle
upon thy weapon; and it shall be, when thou wilt ease
thyself abroad, thou shalt dig therewith, and shalt turn
back and cover that which cometh from thee: For the
LORD *thy God walketh in the midst of thy camp, to*
deliver thee, and to give up thine enemies before
thee; therefore shall thy camp be holy: that he see no
unclean thing in thee, and turn away from thee.
(Deut. 23:12–14)

We are working our way through a biblical home, and as we
come to the bathroom, the universal response of readers is
perhaps less than enthusiastic. And all God's people said,
"Oh, dear." There are reasons for this response, and those
reasons are at the center of the reason for this chapter.

The holiness of God extends to *everything*. We are not
to understand the holiness of God as something merely
"spiritual." Neither should we understand it as some Old
Covenant "ceremonial" thing. The holiness of God is
wholistic in nature, and it encompasses all that God's people
are and all that they do. Notice in the text above that God
could be offended because of a failure to obey Him in the
area of sewage disposal. The army of Israel could be de-
feated in battle because of their latrine policies. Whatever
you do, Scripture says, do it all to the glory of God. We are

fond of saying that the Lordship of Christ extends into everything. Well, here is a place for us to test our mettle.

THREE LAVERS

The bathroom is a room set aside primarily for cleansing. The reason for this is there is always some form of dirt collecting on us or in us that must be removed. Further, removing it is a constant and perpetual task, undertaken on a daily basis. That is what the three "lavers" in the bathroom are dedicated to, whether you are brushing teeth, taking a shower, or using the toilet. These lavers are the sink, the tub, and the toilet.

Incidentally, because the bathroom is a room *dedicated* to cleansing, it's a good place to measure the level of understanding within a household concerning the importance of cleanliness overall. It could be argued that the bathroom should be the cleanest room in the house, but the truth is often the reverse of this. When you are not sure about whether a restaurant is committed to cleanliness, the simplest place to check is one of their bathrooms. What should be cleaner than the place for cleaning?

THREE LAVERS IN PRIVATE

As we approach God in worship, one of the first things we do is confess our sins. We are making ourselves presentable prior to presenting ourselves before Him. In the bathroom, we are performing an analogous service for our neighbor, whom we must love as we love ourselves. The motivation for this must not be vanity, but rather love. My life for yours.

The privacy we seek out for these duties is a universal instinct, and the reason for it is not hard to find. We need the protections of clothes, doors, or social conventions as we acknowledge we are not in Eden. Much of this goes back to shame—not shame over sin, but shame over our fallenness. We are not ashamed of having bodies, but rather of having *fallen* bodies. The soil needs more preparation now, and weeds afflict us. We are *preparing* to love others, and we cannot *do* a thing at the same time we are *preparing* to do it.

CLEANLINESS *IS* NEXT TO GODLINESS

Certain proverbs that come from your great-grandmother or *Poor Richard's Almanac* are often thought to be from somewhere in the Bible. "God helps those who help themselves" is one such proverb, and "cleanliness is next to godliness" is another. While neither are from the Bible, there are important biblical truths contained in each.

Cleanliness is not the same thing as godliness, but it's *next* to godliness. As we consider this, we have to take care to avoid two problems. The first is a reductionist approach that assumes God taught Israel hygiene by means of a trick—by sneaking modern medical truths into the sugar pill of useless ceremonies. This approach assumes that all God was interested in with Old Testament law was dealing with germs. The other error separates the "medical" from the spiritual or ceremonial and sees many of these biblical requirements as "just" sacramental. After all, the blood on Aaron's ear lobe didn't ward off any virus. But it's difficult to avoid seeing that the Mosaic law would leave any people a lot cleaner than it found them, and we know this has direct medical benefits.

One blessing of the Old Covenant economy was *soap*. In the red heifer sacrifice, we have an interesting set-up. The heifer was burnt completely, along with cedar wood (Num. 19:6). We have resulting from this sacrifice two essential ingredients of soap: tallow and wood ash. The remains of the sacrifice were to be used by the Israelites in the waters of cleansing as they prepared for worship (Num. 19:9). There are other aspects of this ritual that might be called "purely" ceremonial, but our goal should be to keep things together. In other words, the ashes of the heifer were taken outside the camp, and the Israelites used these ashes to cleanse themselves as they prepared for worship in the tabernacle. Another way of stating this is that in Israel *ceremonial* cleanliness was the same thing as cleanliness.

This had a relation to the question of *disease*. God told the people of Israel plainly that obedience to all His commandments and statutes would result in them having *none of the diseases* of Egypt (Exod. 15:26). Pagan societies are filthy and consequently disease-ridden. This is an important means of loving our neighbor. Children need to be taught the importance of cleanliness so they don't spread the flu throughout the neighborhood. Of course, we cannot catch everything, but patterns of cleanliness do prevent disease. One of the reasons many families are recurrently sick has more to do with their use of soap than it does their use of vitamins.

Another consideration is simply a question of *manners*. This would include brushing teeth, combing hair, and washing the body—all these are all forms of giving to others. Few things are more difficult than trying to deal charitably with someone who stinks. Some forms of this are constant in every godly society, and some forms vary according to fashion. Parting hair on the side or in the middle is a simple matter of custom. But trying to cultivate that rebellion-lite look is *not* just a matter of custom. All forms of bodily care are forms of communication to others, and love for others is to be at the heart of that communication. Some forms of bodily care are universal just as the smile is universal. Filthiness and squalor are wrong forms of communication regardless of the culture. Wearing neckties is not universal in this sense. But in either case, the need to love one another is to be at the center.

CONCLUSION

The polite averting of the gaze, and the welcoming of the closed bathroom door are fundamental Christian duties.

But this can only be done safely if we take care to guard our imagination. Social taboos can enable us to give to one another, as in this case. We grant privacy to others so they might prepare to give to us, and they grant us the same privilege. But when idolatrously wielded, social taboos can make us fall into rationalistic folly.

This has to be said with great reverence and care, but in the incarnation of Jesus Christ, we have the eternal Word of God taking on flesh—along with all the consequences of this. We reject docetism in all its forms; Jesus had air in His lungs, food in His stomach, and dirt on His hands. Whatever the first century equivalents of our three lavers were, He used them.

CHAPTER TWENTY

The Proverbial Woodshed

But if ye be without chastisement, whereof all are partakers, then are ye bastards, and not sons. Furthermore we have had fathers of our flesh which corrected us, and we gave them reverence: shall we not much rather be in subjection unto the Father of spirits, and live? For they verily for a few days chastened us after their own pleasure; but he for our profit, that we might be partakers of his holiness. Now no chastening for the present seemeth to be joyous, but grievous: nevertheless afterward it yieldeth the peaceable fruit of righteousness unto them which are exercised thereby. Wherefore lift up the hands which hang down, and the feeble knees; And make straight paths for your feet, lest that which is lame be turned out of the way; but let it rather be healed. (Heb. 12:8–13)

No home can function in a scriptural way without discipline. In fact, some form of discipline is inescapable; children are *always* being disciplined and directed. The only question is whether or not the standard that governs this discipline is a scriptural one or not.

In our text, the discipline the Lord gives to all His true sons is compared to the kind of discipline that exists in the home. Note first that refusal to discipline is considered a type of rejection or disowning. The one who spares the rod *hates* his son, Scripture says (Prov. 13:24). Second, human fathers receive reverence as a result of discipline; how much more is God like this? Third, discipline is directional;

it has a particular end in view. Those who discipline in wisdom must always have this end in view; those who are disciplined will grow to understand that end when they have attained it. As a result of this process, we should be encouraged. God disciplines us for our blessing. And it's the responsibility of Christian parents to conform what they do with their children as closely as possible to what God does with His children.

QUALIFICATIONS TO DISCIPLINE
The Scriptures say that if someone is caught up in a trespass, as children frequently are, the one who is spiritual should do the restoring (Gal. 6:1). He should consider himself lest he also be tempted. This means whenever a parent feels like clobbering one of the kids, *he is not qualified to do so.* But whenever he *is* qualified, the emotional motivation is somehow not there. This means the motivation must be obedience to the Word of God and not for the sake of a "little peace and quiet around here."

This is an important part of remembering that less emphasized portion of Eph. 6:4, "provoke not your children to wrath." A good way to provoke wrath is to give way to it yourself (Col. 3:21).

THE OCCASION OF DISCIPLINE
Parents who discipline properly are teaching their children the fundamental principles of biblical justice. What we have just considered is an important part of this. The judge in the robe behind the bench is not supposed to lose his temper and throw things. Justice is to be meted out, not thrown. Justice is calm.

Some other basic principles should be recalled as well: Sorting things out requires two or three witnesses (Deut. 19:15; 2 Cor. 13:1). As a parent, if you saw it yourself you may discipline. But if the case is *brought* to you by someone or some circumstance, the Bible requires independent confirmation of the charge. If you are stymied in a particular instance, always remember God knows *all* the details.

Second, the accuser must be submitted to accountability himself (Deut. 19:19). Always remember tattling and slander require discipline as well (Lev. 19:16).

And third, discipline deals with the heart but not because you can see the heart directly. The matters you discipline for should be "investigatable" in principle (Deut. 19:18). This does not exclude *externalized* attitudes, but it does exclude surmised motives.

THE METHODS OF DISCIPLINE

The family code should be simple and consistent. Erratic discipline is another way to exasperate the children. The code I recall from my childhood was straightforward. "No disobedience. No lying. No disrespecting your mother." Life was simple. And when discipline is applied, it consists of two basic elements.

The first is *pain*. We have already seen that no discipline seems pleasant at the time but rather grievous (Heb. 12:11). If it's not painful, dreaded by the recipient, then it's not discipline. Tippy-tapping on top of the diapers doesn't cut it.

The second element is *restitution*. Discipline differs from punishment in this respect. Discipline is corrective; punishment is retributive. The execution of a murderer is not in order to make him better. It might have that effect, but that's not the point of it. In contrast, the sole point of disciplining your own children is to correct them. It's like giving them a bath; you want *them* to be clean. But correction requires honest restitution (Lk. 19:8).

THE DIRECTION OF DISCIPLINE

Discipline is teleological; wise discipline must keep the end in view. If the result of discipline is a harvest, it makes sense to speak of plowing, planting, tending, and so forth. One procedure doesn't fit every circumstance. Discipline of a two-year-old looks completely different than discipline of a sixteen-year-old.

The central thing to remember is the transition from *artificial* consequences to *natural* consequences. When a child is equipped to live on his own, avoiding sin and the natural consequences of it, that child has acquired self-government, which is the entire point.

For the parents, this means close oversight when children are young, with a purposeful removal of external requirements as the child grows older and more mature. But a word of caution should be offered to the teenagers at this point. The point is maturity, not selfishness.

CHAPTER TWENTY-ONE

The Bills Desk

Be thou diligent to know the state of thy flocks, and look well to thy herds. For riches are not for ever: and doth the crown endure to every generation? The hay appeareth, and the tender grass sheweth itself, and herbs of the mountains are gathered. The lambs are for thy clothing, and the goats are the price of the field. And thou shalt have goats' milk enough for thy food, for the food of thy household, and for the maintenance for thy maidens. (Prov. 27:23–27)

Whenever we want to know what is really going on in any sphere, one of our proverbial exhortations urges us to "follow the money." There is a great deal of wisdom in this, as we shall see when we turn to the Scriptures.

Our passage begins with an exhortation to diligence. In particular, this diligence is to be exerted in the direction of knowing the state of your business. The effect of the command is not to "have money" but rather to *know* what money you have. Diligence in this respect doesn't exclude "seeking first the kingdom" (Mt. 6:33) because the next verse tells us the reason we are to be diligent in our business is precisely *because* riches are not forever. Crops come and go, harvests come and go, and in the meantime, the flocks will supply your needs for both clothing and food. This echoes the wisdom of Ecclesiasties—you should be on top of your finances *because it is all vanity*. Avoid the idolatry of covetousness which tracks money in the foolish belief that it is ultimately important. Avoid the idolatry of ease which refuses to track it in the foolish belief that laziness is ultimately important.

GUARD THE HEART

It's easy to *say*, "God doesn't mind His people having money; He minds money having His people." This is quite true, but saying the correct thing is not the same thing as being free of covetousness. A covetous man is an idolater (Eph. 5:5). It is easier for a camel to get through the eye of a needle than for a rich man to enter the kingdom of heaven (Mt. 19:24–25). We (a *nation* of rich people) wonder what He could possibly have meant by *that*. The love of money is the root cause of all kinds of evil (1 Tim. 6:10). Paul goes on to tell Timothy what to teach the rich people in his congregations.

> Charge them that are rich in this world, that they be not highminded, nor trust in uncertain riches, but in the living God, who giveth us richly all things to enjoy; That they do good, that they be rich in good works, ready to distribute, willing to communicate; Laying up in store for themselves a good foundation against the time to come, that they may lay hold on eternal life. (1 Tim. 6:17–19)

Precisely because we are a nation of rich people, these are words for all of us. Those who are rich are not to be snobs, are not to trust in their wealth, and are to *enjoy* their wealth. There also should be parity between their monetary riches and their rich good works. They are to be generous and willing to share. They are to do all this with a dedicated view of eternal life.

On a related point that needs to be unpacked in much greater detail, many of our cultural dislocations are the result of this odd circumstance we find ourselves in. We are a rich people and yet, because we grade these things on a curve, and we don't travel in the Third World much, we don't know we are incredibly wealthy. When Paul gave this admonition to the "rich in this present world," he was speaking to a small sliver of the population. But these words apply to the vast majority of American households—and yet we don't think they do. We feel no obligation to heed the warnings of Scripture aimed straight at us—we assume that God is speaking here to Bill Gates or Donald Trump.

APPLICATIONS OF THE GUARDED HEART

Questions surrounding our use of money are many, and it must be confessed that some of them are not easy. When we come to the applications of "being diligent to know the state of our herds," we have to confess that in some of these areas the Bible is plain and we are muddled. In others, the question itself is not so easy, but Scripture still requires us to give ourselves to such a question in such a way as to gain wisdom. Some of what follows below should be thought of as initial steps in that process.

The first consideration is the tithe. The tithe existed before the law (Heb. 7:2), during the time of the law (Mal. 3:10), and during the time of the New Covenant (1 Cor. 9:13–14). The requirement is that a tenth of the *increase* be given to the work of the kingdom of God, with particular emphasis placed on supporting the ministry of the Word and sacrament, that is, the local church (Gal. 6:6). Other lawful recipients of the tithe would include the poor (Deut. 14:29) and religious festivals (Deut. 14:22–29). A religious festival, incidentally, doesn't include birthdays and weddings. The principle is that those who sow sparingly, reap sparingly (2 Cor. 9:6).

The tithe is nowhere fulfilled in the New Testament in the same way that the sacrificial system was. This by itself should be sufficient to show us that Christians should honor God by honoring the tithe.

Do ye not know that they which minister about
holy things live of the things of the temple? and
they which wait at the altar are partakers with the
altar? Even so hath the Lord ordained that they
which preach the gospel should live of the gospel.
(1 Cor. 9:13–14)

Paul says that in the Old Testament, the Levites who
ministered in the holy things lived off the things of the
Temple—in short, they lived off the tithe. Those priests
who labored at the altar partook of the altar. In the same
way, Paul says, ministers of the gospel should live off the
gospel. In other words, "even so" the tithe should fund
New Covenant ministers just as it did Old Covenant ministers. This means learning how to tithe is one of the basic
duties of Christian household financial management.

The second great commandment is similar—*pay your
bills*. This is what it means to love your neighbor. It means
that all your debts are to be fully consistent with the debt
of love (Rom. 13:8). This doesn't prohibit fully collateral-
ized debts (e.g., a loan on a house), but it does prohibit
extending your arm farther than you can draw it back. It is
far too easy to say it's a "big company" that routinely ac-
cepts the reality of late payments, and so on. They do the
same thing for shoplifting. The fact that large companies
have to count on a certain number of people sinning against
them is no argument for a Christian to join the throng.
Christians should therefore pay their bills on time. If this
is not possible, then it's necessary to make all appropriate
arrangements with the creditor. Remember, the creditor is
in charge of the arrangements, not the debtor (Prov. 22:7).
So under such difficult circumstances, every conversation
about the debt should be *initiated by the debtor*.

A related financial issue is payment of taxes. The teaching of the New Testament is very clear on this. We as Christians are to *pay our taxes*. The saints in the New Testament
were confronted with life under an unbelieving empire, one
far worse than our unbelieving empire. And those early

Christians were told this:

> For this cause pay ye tribute also: for they are God's
> ministers, attending continually upon this very
> thing. Render therefore to all their dues: tribute to
> whom tribute is due; custom to whom custom;
> fear to whom fear; honour to whom honour.
> (Rom. 13:6–7)

The glibness with which some conservative Christians have
embraced "tax revolt" is truly shameful. Always beware of
legal research done by someone who has established a separate republic of his own that looks an awful lot like a mobile home park in east Texas.

But we have to carry ourselves with wisdom. Faithful
Christians will frequently find themselves in conflict with
idolatrous political power, and sometimes, the money issues
are tangled up in it. But even under the extreme circumstances when this happens, the issue should be idolatry
and not money. Remember the example of Gideon in this
(Judg. 6:11).

Another important financial consideration for every
biblical household is the question of insurance. Given the
hard realities of our modern economy, we should consider
the provision of insurance as a part of providing for a household (1 Tim. 5:8).

Some might object to the corruption of the system and
point out that the purchase of insurance is financially indis-
tinguishable from gambling. Insurance is kind of a negative
lottery. The insurance company does a bunch of research
on whether you are likely to have a heart attack or to have
your house burn down. With their research firmly in place
they approach you and offer to bet that they are wrong.
They rarely are, and this is why more money flows to the
insurance company than flows from it. This is the only kind
of company you would want to buy insurance from. A man
would hardly want to buy insurance from a company about
to become insolvent. But if he buys from a solvent company, then the chances are outstanding that he will send far

more money to them than they will send to him. There are exceptions, of course, which is why people play the lottery. Occasionally, we see someone jumping around excitedly at the 7-11 exclaiming that they won. This keeps the rest of the chumps encouraged to continue.

If there is no financial difference between buying insurance and gambling for fun, then why I am in favor of the former and opposed to the latter? The answer is, with regard to the former, we live in the casino and are forced to place bets. With the latter, I have a real choice. But with the former, I could be driving happily down the road one minute and wake up the next in a hospital bed with $125,000 already racked up. Christian economists and financial experts should work on what a godly system of insurance would look like down the road when we finally get our act together. But in the meantime, we have to provide for our families in this economy, and there is no way to do this responsibly without insurance.

Others might say that to purchase insurance shows that the individual is not "trusting God." But this is also an argument against jobs, bank accounts, clothes, and cars. People can trust in their jobs instead of in God, but the solution is not to quit the job. The solution is to repent and work at the job in an attitude of thanksgiving to God. It's the same with insurance. Besides, many who reject insurance in favor of trusting God are actually putting the burden to provide for them (if disaster strikes) on family and friends.

Having said this, we must distinguish lack of provision (through lack of insurance) through honest poverty and lack of provision (through lack of insurance) through negligence and lack of foresight.

Another financial issue is *savings*. Setting aside a certain portion against the future is wise on two counts. (By a "certain portion" I mean 5-10%). First, the Scriptures commend this kind of wisdom in particular. "The sluggard will not plow by reason of the cold; therefore shall he beg in harvest, and have nothing" (Prov. 20:4). Prepare in season for that which will happen out of season. A pattern of saving is a hedge against future contingencies, whether expected or unexpected.

Second, the pattern of saving establishes the possibility of loving your children and grandchildren through the inheritance you provide. "A good man leaveth an inheritance to his children's children: and the wealth of the sinner is laid up for the just" (Prov. 13:22). This may seem obvious, but unless the inheritance is set aside or laid up it will not be there for subsequent generations. And if a couple start saving in their sixties, it's unlikely what they do will amount to much. A thoughtful provision this way should begin a long time before.

CONCLUSION

Returning to our text quoted at the beginning of this chapter, we need to understand information is *golden*. In most cases, what is needed is information, not money. Many people have three times more money than you do and are in the same kind of trouble. They just have a *bigger* sinking boat. "Be diligent to know the state of thy flocks." Most financial blunders are made in the dark, and whether the darkness was innocent or culpable does not alter the result.

Epilogue: My Life for Yours

I beseech you therefore, brethren, by the mercies of God, that ye present your bodies a living sacrifice, holy, acceptable unto God, which is your reasonable service. And be not conformed to this world: but be ye transformed by the renewing of your mind, that ye may prove what is that good, and acceptable, and perfect, will of God. For I say, through the grace given unto me, to every man that is among you, not to think of himself more highly than he ought to think; but to think soberly, according as God hath dealt to every man the measure of faith. (Rom. 12:1–3)

As we conclude our consideration of the biblical home, please allow just a few more words on the central theme of Christian living in a Christian home.

We are very familiar with the first two verses here but sometimes do not connect them to the verse following. We are to present our bodies as a living sacrifice to God—my life for yours—and this is to be considered as entirely reasonable. It is not an "above and beyond" kind of thing. We are not to be shaped by the world but rather to be transformed in our thinking so that we can do what is good, acceptable, and perfect. In short, we are to do the will of God. And then comes the cash payout—if we do this, refusing the mold of the world, we will think of ourselves *soberly*, in *faith*. Every Christian must learn this lesson and learn it well. Think of your behavior in your home soberly and without inflation. Walk by faith, not by self-esteem.

Self-centeredness is always destructive, and it always destroys in monotonously similar ways. Charity, in its turn, always brings about a harvest of kindness and mercy. This is why all familial questions should never be addressed apart from the question, "Has it been *my life for yours*?"

Scripture Index

Ruth

1:20–21 — 42

1 Samuel

1:10 — 42

2 Samuel

7:12 — 78

1 Kings

6:3 — 9

2 Kings

12:9 — 10
21:13 — 38

1 Chronicles

4:40 — 57
26:18–19 —
    107
28:11 — 9

Nehemiah

8:10 — 57
9:25 — 34, 57
9:35 — 57

Esther

9:26–27 — 29

Job

15:27 — 57
31:9–12 — 12

Psalms

4:4–5 — 80
4:8 — 80
10:2–4 — 25
16:11 — 75
17:10 — 57
22:29 — 57
34:2 — 26
36:8 — 57
64:2–4 — 44
65:11 — 57
73:6–7 — 24
73:7 — 57
92:12–14 —
    57
116:10 — 85
116:10–19 —
    85
116:11 — 86
116:12 — 86
116:13–14 —
    86
116:15 — 86
116:16 — 86
116:17 — 86
116:18–19 —
    86
119:70 — 57
123:2 — 93

Proverbs

3:21–26 — 77
3:24 — 78
5:3–4 — 44
5:8 — 14
5:19 — 75
6:9–11 — 78
6:16–17 — 24
7:1–23 — 73
7:7 — 75
7:10 — 73
7:11 — 74
7:13 — 74
7:18 — 74
7:21 — 74
7:22–23 — 75
8:13 — 25
9:13–14 — 14
11:2 — 25
11:25 — 57
13:4 — 57
13:22 — 155
13:24 — 145
14:4 — 20
16:18 — 25
17:1 — 33, 36
18:13 — 118
18:17 — 118
19:15 — 79
20:4 — 154
20:5 — 114
20:13 — 79
22:7   — 152
23:19–21 —
    56
24:30–34 —
    79

27:23–27 — 149
28:7 — 56
28:25 — 57
29:23 — 25
31 — 14
31:12–13 — 132
31:21–22 — 131
31:22 — 135

Ecclesiastes

5:12 — 80
7:4 — 89

Song of Solomon

5:1 — 75

Isaiah

5:20 — 44
6:10 — 57
10:16 — 57
25:6 — 57
29:10 — 78
55:2 — 57
58:11 — 57
60:11 — 11

Jeremiah

2:19 — 43
4:17–18 — 43
5:28 — 57

49:31 — 11

Ezekiel

16:49 — 24
38:11 — 11

Daniel

4:34–37 — 26

Joel

2:17 — 9

Malachi

2:14–15 — 67
3:10 — 151

Matthew

10:25 — 13
13:27 — 13
13:52 — 13
15:17 — 57
19:24–25 — 150
20:1 — 13
20:11 — 13
21:33 — 13
22:11–12 — 133
23:5 — 135
23:25 — 92
23:26 — 101
24:43 — 13

25:10 — 12

Mark

3:5 — 61
7:7–8 — 31
7:18–19 — 54
7:22–23 — 24
11:15–17 — 61

Luke

10:38–42 — 36
15:13 — 56
18:11 — 104
19:8 — 147
22:62 — 42

John

3:36 — 62
10:1–2 — 12
10:7–10 — 12
10:22 — 29
13:4 — 133
13:12 — 133
21:7 — 133

Acts

8:18–23 — 43
16:15 — 66
20:7 — 47
20:38 — 87

Romans

3:14 — 45
5:9–10 — 64
12:1–2 — 19,
65, 77, 92
12:1–3 — 157
12:9 — 98
12:9–13 — 97
12:10 — 59
12:13 — 98
12:19 — 62
13:4 — 62
13:6 — 62
13:6–7 — 153
13:8 — 59,
152
13:11 — 78
14:13 — 59
15:7 — 59
15:14 — 59
16:18 — 57

1 Corinthians

4:7 — 26
5:7–8 — 48
5:9–13 — 99
5:45 — 51
6:9 — 55
6:13–56 — 55
6:18–20 — 55
7:2–3 — 75
9:13–14 —
151, 152
10:7–8 — 105
15:55–57 —
87

16:2 — 47

2 Corinthians

4:17 — 87
9:6 — 151
10:17 — 26
13:1 — 118,
146

Galatians

5:6 — 35
5:13 — 35
5:20 — 62
5:21 — 62
6:1 — 109,
146
6:6 — 151

Ephesians

2:8–10 — 82
4:26 — 42, 62
4:30–31 — 43
4:30–32 — 61
4:31 — 42
5:4 — 104
5:5 — 150
5:14 — 78
6:1 — 91
6:4 — 124,
146

Philippians

2:1 — 17

2:1–4 — 17
2:2 — 18
2:3 — 18
2:4 — 18
2:12–13 — 82
3:18–19 — 57
4:6–7 — 81
4:8–9 — 101
4:9 — 104
4:11 — 84

Colossians

2:20–23 — 57
3:5 — 71
3:8 — 63
3:19 — 44
3:20 — 91
3:21 — 146

1 Thessalonians

4:13 — 87
4:14 — 78

2 Thessalonians

3:12 — 80

1 Timothy

2:9 — 72, 135
3:2 — 97
3:6 — 26
4:1–5 — 53
5:8 — 153
5:14 — 13

6:10 — 150
6:17–19 —
    150

2 Timothy

2:22 — 74
4:7–8 — 88

Titus

2:4–5 — 13

Hebrews

2:14 — 87
3:7–8 — 94
4:9–10 — 47
5:14 — 102
7:2 — 151
11:22 — 89
12 — 45
12:8–13 —
    145

12:11 — 118,
    147
12:14–15 —
    43
13:1 — 65
13:1–2 — 99
13:1–5 — 65
13:2 — 65
13:3 — 65
13:4 — 65, 75
13:5 — 65, 66

James

1:20 — 63
2:2–3 — 135
2:26 — 37
3:11–14 — 45

1 Peter

2:11 — 74
3:1–6 — 27
3:3–4 — 135
4:8–9 — 99

5:6–7 — 81

1 John

1:9 — 45
2:15–17 — 23,
    136
5:21 — 54

2 John

10–11 — 99

3 John

8 — 99

Jude

11–12 — 48

Revelation

1:10 — 47
21:25 — 11